IF WALLS COULD TALK

Manitoba's Best Buildings Explored & Explained

DAVID BUTTERFIELD & MAUREEN DEVANIK BUTTERFIELD

GREAT PLAINS
PUBLICATIONS

Great Plains Publications
420-70 Arthur Street
Winnipeg, MB R3B 1G7
www.greatplains.mb.ca

Great Plains Publications gratefully acknowledges the financial support provided
for its publishing program by the Government of Canada through the Book
Publishing Industry Development Program (BPIDP); the Canada Council for the Arts;
and the Manitoba Department of Culture, Heritage and Citizenship; and the
Manitoba Arts Council.

Design & Typography by Taylor George Design

Printed in Canada by Kromar Printing

CANADIAN CATALOGUING IN PUBLICATION DATA

Butterfield, David K. (David Kenneth), 1955 –

If walls could talk

ISBN 1-894283-11-2

1.   Architecture(Manitoba(History.   I.   Butterfield, Maureen Devanik.

II. Title.

NA746.M3B88   2000   720.97127   C00-920007-X

TO OUR PARENTS, DORIS AND FLOYD, TANNIS AND STANLEY

TABLE OF CONTENTS

PREFACE

A VACANT, BROKEN-DOWN MANITOBA FARM HOUSE is a Prairie icon, symbolic of a time passed and a people vanished. Such places, however, are more than just symbols. They are embodiments of time, space and culture. Step through the weathered door of that farmhouse, in the heat of a late July day, and you can feel the chill of abandonment and smell the dust settled there. Tread carefully, because the floors may be rotting and spongy to the step. Shafts of light try to poke through the faded, ragged curtains that ominously flap over yellowed windows. The surrounding quiet is sharp and hard, like the broken glass shards covering the floor. Except for you, no one's been here for years.

A simple object, like a glass left lying on a counter, is a reminder that once the cupboards of this house were filled with dinnerware, the walls were dappled with sunlight and the air was sweet with the smells of home-cooked meals. The structure has endured, but its occupants are long gone. Why did they leave? Were they driven out by a failed crop or the need for more space? Were they wealthy, or poor? When they left, they took their belongings, stories and history. All that's left are their secrets.

My partner David's love of the mystery and loneliness of abandoned farmhouses solidified his interest in architectural history. As a youth living in Brandon, Manitoba, he would roam the countryside looking for lost buildings. Old farmhouses and deserted churches were the setting for his explorations. Once inside he wondered how something so public, so visible, and so enduring could shroud the very essence of the people who lived there and the culture that inhabited it.

Today, his profession as an architectural historian gives him the chance to work in an area of great personal interest. It is, moreover, his passion for needing to know more about architecture than its styles, building materials, and social history, that lead to this book. It's also his interest in people, those who influenced, designed, built or inhabited buildings, coupled with a love of researching and investigating the past. In my work as an Internet publisher, my days are spent focused firmly on structures that are virtual. Immersed all day long in the electronic storefront, my interest in physical buildings continues to grow.

We wanted to include more buildings than are in this book. Here, readers will see the final cut, an eclectic mix of some of Manitoba's finest buildings, and may wonder why a certain building was not discussed. Simply put, there were not enough pages to cover all of Manitoba's premiere buildings, so we decided to emphasize the best of our older buildings. But we did not approach the final list in a random manner.

Some buildings profiled in this book were chosen to trace Manitoba's history; illuminating the sequence of events that shaped its past. For example, the lives of First Peoples are introduced in Tipi; the experiences of explorers and fur traders in the 18th century are suggested in Prince of Wale's Fort; the triumphs of the first settlers are revealed in Kennedy House; the struggles of the immigrants who arrived in the late 19th century can be sensed in the buildings at the Negrycz Farm; the first hint of the opportunities of the agricultural economy is evident in the Sandison Farm; the province's gradual maturing, its proud entry onto the Canadian stage as a wealthy and sophisticated player can be read in buildings as diverse as the Legislative Building, Macdonald House (Dalnavert), Isaac Brock School, Westminster United Church, Hotel Fort Garry and the Electric Railway Chambers Building. Other buildings were chosen because they are architecturally or historically significant. Their inclusion may seem to cover well-traveled ground, but in those cases we have attempted to cast them in new light by revealing something about them that has not previously been published or is not widely known.

In all of our decisions we were compelled by architecture first – designs, styles, philosophies, materials and technology. However, this book is not meant to be an academic treatment of architectural history, and we admit to being moved by the stories of the people behind the walls. While researching we encountered intriguing and surprising stories about the lives of writers, politicians, and entrepreneurs. We have conveyed how all buildings ultimately reflect people, because after all, people make them.

So when we look at the architecture of farm buildings, another story will unfold – that of the resilience and inventiveness that often characterized those first settlers of Manitoba. When we review the adoption of new architectural styles, and the increasing facility employed with new materials, we animate the sophistication of architects, builders and clients in a particular era. We embed sub-plots about great wealth and ambition, and of poverty and struggle. We depict how love of God can define architectural design. In each case we have tried to illustrate the human condition via stories about buildings.

We also demonstrate how to undertake a research project for a home or a building. This section is intended for beginner researchers who may be inspired to undertake their own architectural detective work after reading this book. We list sources of information and identify what things to look for, alongside a case history of research for our own home.

Maureen Devanik Butterfield
David Butterfield

WINNIPEG, JUNE 2000

Chapter 1

HOMES

Tipi

IN THE DEAD OF A MANITOBA WINTER, when it's 40 degrees below zero, the wind is howling and the night is pitch black, some wonder, "How did Native people do it? How did they live through this brutal weather without solid walls and furnaces?"

It was accomplished with an ancient building tradition—the tipi—that was so flexible it allowed for a great variety of responses to whatever the weather would throw at them.

The tipi was well-suited to the lifestyle of nomadic hunters and gatherers living on the plains. It was lightweight and therefore easily transported, and constructed entirely of locally available materials: wood for poles, animal skins, bark and grasses. Comprised of fragile, natural elements, tipi materials decomposed easily and it is not surprising that no original tipis have survived.

The origin of the tipi in Manitoba is cloudy, but may date from as early as 10,000 B.C., when people first inhabited the province. Archaeological evidence indicates that tipis were definitely constructed by 5,000 B.C.

Tipis and tipi villages would have stood, however briefly, wherever food sources were available. Thus water courses and lakes (for fish) and sheltered valleys (for bison and berries) would have been frequently occupied sites.

The form of the tipi was a tilted cone, with the steep side at the rear of the structure set into the prevailing wind. The frame consisted of a series of tree poles, trimmed and stripped of bark. The tipi usually consisted of an outer cover of heavy material and a thinner inner liner. Tipi coverings were originally hides, bark, or mats made out of rushes, and after the 1880s, canvas. Rocks, sod or wooden pegs were used to anchor coverings to the ground. An opening was created at the top, with flaps to direct the smoke.

The tipi was resilient in all kinds of weather. During windstorms ropes were stretched over the outside of the frame to anchor the building. When thunderstorms beat down, guide poles outside the tipi allowed occupants to close the smoke flaps to keep the interior dry. On sweltering hot days the tipi hem was lifted up and propped on sticks to provide entry for cooling breezes. In winter, the pocket between the inner liner and outer cover was stuffed with grasses and snow was banked outside to provide insulation. With a fire raging, the interior was completely comfortable. Wearing furs on the coldest nights, the occupants were entirely warm.

EARLY WOMEN ARCHITECTS AND BUILDERS

The tipi was not only a refuge, but was the focus for spiritual expression, shrouded with ceremony and ritual. The doorway almost always faced the rising sun and sacred medicine bundles often hung on wooden tripods inside. The oldest male occupant usually slept at the back of the tipi. Some groups, particularly the Sioux of western Manitoba, painted the outside covering with symbols and patterns to recall events and spiritual activity. Such paintings, however, could not be applied without permission of the women. It was they who not only constructed the tipi, repaired it and erected it at each new camp site, the women owned the tipis.

PENNER HOUSE

The simple elegant shape of the tipi, in its original Manitoba form often built with animal skins and bark, has been re-energized by contemporary architect David Penner in the design of his own house. The silver cone rises like the ghost of an ancient building tradition in a neighbourhood—Winnipeg's Crescentwood—that is a haven for Edwardian mansions of stone and brick.

Penner House photo courtesy of Roger Brooks

Grey Nuns' Convent

The Grey Nuns' Convent, built between 1846 and 1851 to the designs of L'Abbe Louis-Francois Lafleche, is thought to be the largest log building constructed in North America. Now St. Boniface Museum, it is the oldest building in Winnipeg and the oldest residential structure in western Canada.

THE FOUR ROMAN CATHOLIC NUNS who departed from Montreal for St. Boniface in 1844 must have been of hardy stock and prepared for adversity as they contemplated their duties, serving the Roman Catholic population at the Red River Settlement. Otherwise, how would they have endured the various obstacles they faced over the ensuing five years as they struggled to create, in the comparative wilderness a place of grace and charity?

Invited by Bishop Joseph Provencher to make the journey west, these nuns of the order of the Sisters of Charity, also called Grey Nuns, first persevered a 2,500 kilometre-journey by canoe and on foot that would have taxed even the most experienced *voyageur*. The warm welcome from the residents of St. Boniface must have been comforting; their lodgings were not: a small log shack with a thatched roof.

Even the promised construction, begun in 1846, of a grand convent building of log construction, adjacent to St. Boniface Cathedral, was not without hardship. In the room in which they were to reside, the chinking—the material stuffed in the gaps between the logs—was not completed, and the women hung thick buffalo robes over the walls in an effort to reduce the cold and the wind.

Reports of early habitation are sketchy, but suggest that the nuns slept directly on the floor, probably on buffalo robes. The only piece of furniture they had, likely left over from construction, was a large plank supported on saw horses, that served as a dining table. Every morning they moved the "table" and their sleeping gear to a corner so they could use the room for other purposes. This daily exercise, of removing the evidence of their own domestic life to accommodate the needs of their community, became a theme in the evolution of the convent. With new services and functions added over the years (school, orphanage, hospital, seniors' home) the sisters' living quarters (by the 1850s more substantial, with beds in a dormitory setting to make room for the increased numbers of nuns) moved regularly within the building to adapt to the changes. The spirit of the order—of loving service for Jesus to the poor—was truly embraced by these kind and determined women.

THE GREY NUNS

Their origins in Manitoba may have been modest, but the Grey Nuns have become a formidable force in the community. The nuns' primary purpose—the education of Catholic children—gradually shifted to the medical needs of St. Boniface. The Grey Nuns established a hospital in 1871, the first in western Canada, a facility that evolved into St. Boniface General Hospital and which still stands today.

Twin Oaks

TWIN OAKS IS STRONG, symmetrical, handsome. Situated on Winnipeg's River Road, it exudes order and class not just in terms of elegance but also in terms of social hierarchy. It represents the pinnacle of early Manitoba architecture—the Georgian style. Buildings in that style were typically erected before 1870 either by the Hudson's Bay Company (HBC) or by members of the established order (retired HBC officers, clergy and the wealthy). The houses connected their owners to the conservative roots of the land-owning gentry of Great Britain and thus conveyed to observers the high social standing of those within. Inside, the comforting symmetry and imposing formality introduced outside was reinforced with spacious rooms opening off broad central halls.

This house was built around 1858 as a girl's school. Retired HBC families contributed about $12,000 (then a princely sum), to pay for construction and furnishing and to underwrite the salary for the headmistress Miss Matilda Davis. Duncan McRae, the settlement's most respected stonemason built the house with stones quarried from the nearby riverbank when the water was low.

TWIN OAKS, THEN AND NOW

When Twin Oaks was photographed around 1890 (above), the stately proportions and sure stonework were evident, but so was the harsh absence of vegetation. By the time of the second photograph (left), lush growth had softened the background and the corners of the building. The house has been carefully maintained over the years and is now a private residence.

Kennedy House

COMPARED TO TWIN OAKS, Kennedy House is awkward and unsure. When it was built (starting in 1866), however, it was one of the first attempts to introduce to the staid Red River Settlement a new and fashionable architectural style—Gothic Revival. Some of the tenets of Gothic architecture, from which Gothic Revival was developed, were not unknown in the Settlement. The pointed window and highly decorated wooden details were commonly used for churches (see St. Andrew's and St. Peter's Anglican churches, pages 54 and 55), but in houses the style was only gaining wide acceptance in England by the early nineteenth century. Its appearance in one of the major new houses at Red River represented, along with political and social changes, the first stirrings of modern life that were beginning to connect Manitoba to the outside world. The same mason who worked on Twin Oaks, Duncan McRae, also laboured at Kennedy House using stones collected from the river bank near St. Andrew's Rapids.

KENNEDY HOUSE, THEN AND NOW

Photographed from the east side of the Red River around 1880 (above) Kennedy House was perched on the riverbank and screened by low trees. By 1985, when it was restored as a museum and tea house (right), a Victorian-style garden had replaced the original landscape.

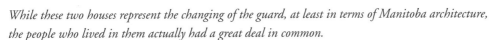

MISS DAVIS, MEET MISTER KENNEDY

While these two houses represent the changing of the guard, at least in terms of Manitoba architecture, the people who lived in them actually had a great deal in common.

William Kennedy, better known as Captain Kennedy, was a larger-than-life character whose exploits were a chronicle of adventure and action in business, exploration and politics. Born in Cumberland House (west of The Pas, in present-day Saskatchewan) in 1814, he was an HBC man, an entrepreneur, and a social and political activist. He left the HBC over a dispute regarding its liquor trade, and in 1851 led the thirteenth search for the lost Arctic explorer Sir John Franklin. He had a powerful sense of himself and of his destiny. At Red River, ensconced at this house, he was a well known and trusted leader.

Matilda Davis was also a child of the HBC. Her brother was the chief factor at Lower Fort Garry. Miss Davis was, like Captain Kennedy, a well educated person and likely spent time at the Kennedy home, more likely in the company of Mary Kennedy, herself an accomplished musician.

Riel House

RIEL HOUSE is one of the most tragic houses in Manitoba. The body of Louis Riel, the famous defender of Métis rights, leader of the Red River Rebellion of 1869-70, and now considered a Father of Confederation, lay in state here in December of 1885 after hanging for the crime of treason following the defeat of his forces in the North-West Rebellion. Riel lay here for two days. On December 12, 1885, a mile-long funeral cortège wound its way into St. Boniface and to St. Boniface Roman Catholic Cathedral. After the funeral Mass, Riel's body was placed in the nearby cemetery next to the burial site of his father Louis Sr.

The tragic connections to Riel House did not end there. Louis's young wife Marguerite died there in May 1886. Their teenage daughter, 14-year old Angélique, succumbed to diphtheria there in 1897. Finally, and sadly their son Jean died nearby in 1897, aged 26, the victim of a buggy accident. Louis's entire family, wiped out tragically. No progeny left to perpetuate his name.

In some ways Riel House began under a peculiar cloud of sad events. The house was built for Julie Riel, Louis's mother, on land granted to her by Bishop Taché, probably in sympathy after the death of her husband Louis Sr. in 1864. Lot 51, in the Parish of St. Vital, bordered on two of Manitoba's best known rivers. The lot stretched right across from the banks of the Red River to those of the Seine. Julie and six of her nine children still living with her, originally built Riel House at the Seine River end of their family lot and commenced farming. During this time Louis was already studying in Quebec. He returned from his education in 1868, and probably took up lodging within the walls of the Seine River location.

In the early 1880s Julie decided to disassemble the house, and moved it for reconstruction to the Red River end of the lot. Louis never lived in Riel House in its new location because, by this time, he was already living on his own. He did stay there briefly in the summer of 1883 while attending his sister Henriette's wedding. But from October of 1869, until his exile from Manitoba at the end of August 1870, when the Red River Rebellion collapsed, his thoughts were often elsewhere, as was he. It was only on those two ice-cold December days in 1885, when Louis's body was laid out for viewing, that he finally rested within Riel House, in its final location.

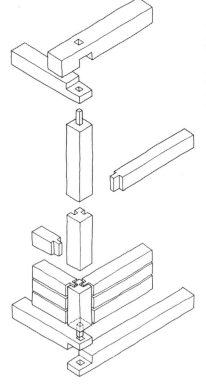

A MANITOBA WAY OF BUILDING

Before 1870 a distinct log construction technology, called Red River frame, was the construction method used by most inhabitants of the Red River Settlement. The procedure was used primarily for houses, but also found favour for public, commercial and religious structures. While the logs often were exposed to the elements, it was also common, especially for houses, to layer on an outside sheath of mud, often mixed with clay, dung and horsehair, or if affordable, wooden siding (as was done at the Riel House). This gave buildings a more polished, finished appearance. The building technique was introduced in western Canada by Hudson's Bay Company employees from Quebec where a similar building methodology was popular. The inspiration for the Quebec buildings was derived from buildings of 17th century France. Red River frame is conversely referred to by its French equivalent pièce-sur-pièce.

The most distinctive feature of Red River frame is the log construction procedure (shown here with a typical corner detail). Short logs, squared and cut at each end with projecting tongues, were set between upright squared logs cut lengthways with mortises. This kept the logs firmly in place. Red River frame does not require nails, and since it consists of interlocking pieces, settlers could easily disassemble a building and move it to another location. This is what Julie Riel undertook when she moved her family's home from the Seine to the Red River. In Manitoba fewer than 20 Red River frame buildings remain, most situated along the banks of the Red and Assiniboine rivers, within the confines of the old Red River Settlement.

An early view of Julie Riel's house

THE RIELS

Louis Riel was from a storied Manitoba family and although his bloodline was extinguished with the death of his son at the young age of 26 (without children), the Riel family itself is still a well known presence in the province.

Louis Riel's mother Julie (1820-1906) was a member of a Red River aristocracy of sorts. Her parents Marie-Anne and Jean-Baptiste Lagimodière were legendary figures in the early life of the West. Jean-Baptiste (1778-1855) was a successful fur trader and Marie-Anne (1782-1875) was the first white woman to live in the wilderness. Their first child (born 1807) Reine, was the first white child born in Manitoba.

In 1844 Julie Lagimodière married Jean-Louis Riel (1817-1864). He was originally from Quebec, but had ties to the West and arrived here in 1843 to take up a teaching post at Saint Boniface. By 1849 the Riels were landowners and successful farmers, and became involved in other economic pursuits, particularly milling. Jean-Louis was also passionately engaged in the settlement's political life becoming a well known and articulate spokesman for the rights of Métis and French inhabitants. But it was their first child Louis (1844-85), who was to change the history of Manitoba.

Louis was smart and in 1858 was granted a scholarship to study in Montreal. When he returned to his mother's house in St. Vital, in July of 1868, he was well-educated. Though he set to work at the family farm, events over the next two years thrust Louis into history. He became the chief spokesman for the cause of Métis rights, led the Red River Rebellion, an armed insurrection to oppose Anglo-Ontarian aggressions, and became President of a Provisional (Red River) Government. While the rebellion was ultimately crushed, Riel's work paid off. When Manitoba formally entered Confederation as a full-fledged province, rather than a colony, Manitobans had Louis to thank.

After his departure from Manitoba, Louis spent several years kicking around the West, finally finding work as a teacher in Montana. In 1883 he married Marguerite Monet (1861-1886) the daughter of a well known Métis family from the White Horse Plains of Manitoba. They had two children Jean and Angélique.

Riel's political work was not quite done. In 1884 he embarked on a final crusade, this time in Saskatchewan. Here, Métis groups were agitating for their rights and in 1885 Riel led an armed insurrection. The North-West Rebellion was crushed at Batoche and Riel was captured, tried and convicted of treason. He was hanged in Regina on 16 November, 1885.

Julie and Jean Riel

THE MÉTIS

Who were the Métis, the people whose cause Louis Riel so passionately defended? Métis is an old French word meaning "mixed." The term is used to describe the offspring of Aboriginal women and French Canadian voyageurs who were arriving in the Northwest by the 1700s. By the end of the 18th century these people had a profound sense of their unique racial roots through a powerful amalgamation of two rich cultures: that of French Canadians and of Aboriginals. Together, a new cultural ethos was formed when aspects such as the Roman Catholic religion and native spirituality, differing first languages, and an abiding connection to the land (the buffalo hunt and portaging) were blended.

A nation was born.

Comparatively, the offspring of English traders and their Aboriginal wives were often referred to as Mixed-bloods and did not as readily identify themselves as a nation of people.

By 1869 the Métis were the dominant group at Red River, not only in terms of population, but also by virtue of their economic successes and the development of a leadership class: well-educated and politically astute. Consequently by 1869, when the Federal Government undertook to colonize the Red River area, the Métis led by Riel fought back. While they suffered various setbacks over the years the Métis persevered and today are a living testament to a rich and unique ancestry.

Government House

ONE BUILDING in Manitoba that is associated with fame and power is Government House. It has felt the footsteps of Winston Churchill, Princess Christina of Sweden and Vigdis Finnbogadottir, a President of Iceland. It has resounded with the voices of Lord and Lady Baden Powell, Sarah Bernhardt, Gracie Fields, Harry Belafonte, Bill Cosby and Sammy Davis Jr. It has also fallen under a hush with the humble grace of moral authorities like Andrei Sakharov and Yelena Bonner, famed Soviet peace activists, and Mother Theresa.

Government House is a symbol of the nation's constitutional heritage and a powerful link to the early political and social life of Manitoba.

The name of the building is not merely a descriptive appellation. It is a reminder of the origins of the province's government. George Simpson, the famous Hudson's Bay Company Governor of Rupert's Land, the huge territory that encompassed what is now Manitoba, made his headquarters at Upper Fort Garry, and his home was officially designated as Government House. In 1872, two years after Manitoba entered Confederation, the house was leased to the Dominion Government as the home of the province's first Lieutenant-Governor Adams G. Archibald.

On January 2, 1871, Lieutenant-Governor Archibald hosted a New Year's Levee at Upper Fort Garry so that the general populace could meet and chat with the Canadian government's new vice-regal representative in Manitoba. The first Levee was held at Government House in 1884 and provided curious citizens with the opportunity to see inside the new house.

The office of the Lieutenant-Governor has changed over time. In early years it was a position of import, with the incumbent empowered to deny bills, and to make and unmake ministries. By the turn of the century the position had assumed a more honorary role, with the nominee fulfilling a role as a social and political leader. This important function in our society has been ably carried out by 21 individuals, 18 of whom actually lived in this house.

Government House was designed by the office of Thomas Scott, Chief Architect the federal Department of Public Work. and was built over the course of ten months, between early September of 1882 and July 1, 1883. It is one of a handful of Second Empire-style buildin that remain in Manitoba. Second Empire was, at that time, one of the mo popular architectural styles in North America, often used by governments to express their power and sophistication. Today the style of Government House stands in marked contrast with other nearby government buildings (the Legislative Building, page 44, Courthouse, Land Titles Office). Where they are deeply sombre structures carried out in Classical Revival styles, and are o monolithic stone construction, Government House is dainty, an antidot to the serious business carried out at the adjacent buildings.

A WILD MAN IN GOVERNMENT HOUSE

Perhaps one of the most famous residents of Government House was John Christian Schultz (1840-1896). Depending on what side you took in the Red River Rebellion of 1869-70, Schultz was either a hero or a villain. He was one of the leaders opposed to Louis Riel and the Métis and their struggle with the Government of Canada, to protect their property and language rights, on the eve of Manitoba's entry into Confederation. Schultz organized the pro-Canadian faction, promoted the entry of Manitoba into Confederation as a colony rather than with full provincial status, and opened doors for Anglo-Ontario settlement. While Riel's side won the day, creating the Province of Manitoba with Métis rights recognized Schultz's side could also claim victory, at least in the long term. Ontario settlers were sweeping into Manitoba in the 1880s, displacing many Métis and challenging the province's bilingual character. That Schultz was Lieutenant Governor for ten years (1885-1895) must have sent Riel spinning in his grave.

Isabel Meighen was standing on the front porch when she heard that her husband had become Prime Minster. Later that day, July 10, 1920, his supporters lit bonfires in front of the house and, because the country was still in the throes of Prohibition, served lemonade to the revelers.

Arthur Meighen House

HE WAS OUR PRIME MINISTER, the only one this province ever produced. Arthur Meighen may not have served for long (from July 10, 1920 to December 29, 1921 and then June 29, 1926 to September 25, 1926, a total of about 20 months), but with the recent brief prime ministerial careers of Joe Clark (nine months), John Turner (three months) and Kim Campbell (four months) his tenure now seems more substantial.

Arthur Meighen was not a native-born Manitoban. Like so many others arriving in the province in the late 19th century, he was from Ontario (a town called Anderson), and as a young man embraced the opportunities offered in the developing West. He arrived in Portage la Prairie in 1896, at the age of 22, and set up shop as a lawyer, a career he would build on for the next 12 years. In 1904 he married Isabel Cox, a local girl, and continued on his lawyerly rise.

The Meighens built their first house, a modest affair but within a few years, and with a family of three children, set their sights on a larger place, in a more exclusive part of town. The house they built was not a mansion, although it was lovingly detailed, with the decorative possibilities of wood carefully exploited. Richly textured bargeboards at the gable ends, ornate brackets under the eaves, patterned sections throughout and a wealth of columns added up to a building whose elegance came on you slowly. Arthur Meighen must have been proud of his fine new home. It reflected his character, apparently modest but brimming with confidence.

PRIME MINISTER ARTHUR MEIGHEN (1874-1960)

Arthur Meighen's political career began in 1908 when he stood for election and secured the federal seat of Portage la Prairie for the Conservative Party. In 1913 he was appointed solicitor general in Borden's government and also served as Minister of the Interior. He was acknowledged to be a masterful parliamentarian, but one who also was deeply partisan and reveled in the sharp adversarial side of the life. In short, he made enemies, and seemed to enjoy doing so. In 1919, as acting Minister of Justice, he was instrumental in ending the Winnipeg General Strike, incurring the enmity of much of the labour movement. When Borden retired in 1920, Meighen went after the leadership, a position that even some Conservative colleagues advised him to decline, suggesting that he was temperamentally unsuited to the job and that he was handicapped by connections to past contentious policies. In retrospect it probably was good advice. The rise of new political party—the Progressives—attracted many voters and the Conservatives went down to defeat in the federal election of 1921. Meighen stayed on as Leader of the Opposition and even rebuilt party fortunes over the next several years. A brief stint again as Prime Minister in 1925, the result of the resignation of the King government over a scandal, was reversed in another general election, but for all intents and purposes Meighen's role in Parliament was over.

Hugh John Macdonald House (Dalnavert)

IN DECEMBER, 1895, shortly after construction on Dalnavert was completed, a writer for the *Winnipeg Tribune* visited Hugh John Macdonald's new residence. In the article "A Perfect House," the scribe took readers on a tour of the home from the point of view of the Macdonald family, Hugh John, his wife and their two children, and noted with pride and pleasure its many attributes.

The writer began at the front door identifying it as being comprised of "Michigan red oak." Next to the vestibule where, "on one side is a large radiator, the floor is of coloured tiles [and] opening a small door, a little compartment [is] revealed with a row of hooks; at the end a porcelain wash basin with water taps and towels, etc., for the gentleman whose fingers have suffered in removing muddy rubbers, what could be more welcome?" He then moves the reader into the hall with its "artistic staircase"; the drawing room where "the whole effect [of which] is white and gold, [and at whose] further end is a Corinthian fireplace"; the study and smoking rooms whose "prevailing tints are rich brown, the wallpaper leather paper and the woodwork oiled cedar"; the "boudoir of the mistress, a bright, sunny little room with an air of perpetual spring about it, white and mauve, the south end all glass"; the dining room "a vision of oak"; upstairs to the private apartments "furnished with artistic wood mantles in oak and sycamore"; and finally into the bathrooms "all with porcelain lined baths, tiled floors and walls, marble washbasins, spray baths, etc."

The impressive tour concluded with the servants' quarters, and the various rooms associated with their lives: sewing rooms, bedding closets, coal cellar, cistern, laundry, drying room, kitchen.

Isolated in a sea of modern apartment blocks and office buildings in downtown Winnipeg, Dalnavert was once part of an enclave of mansions that housed Winnipeg's elite. A bold, yet refined example of Romanesque Revival architecture, it was conceived by Charles Wheeler, one of Winnipeg's best early architects. The house boasted many novel and early conveniences, most distinctly, electricity. When Sir Hugh John Macdonald died in 1929 the house was divided into residential suites. It was restored by the Manitoba Historical Society between 1971 and 1974. Today, it operates as a public museum, impeccably restored and maintained.

ENGLAND = OAK

A quote from the Winnipeg Tribune, *21 December 1895 called* A Perfect House *suggests the chauvinistic tenor of the times:*

"The dining room is reached from the end of the main hall and is, if the expression might be allowed, a vision in oak. This expression, however, must not be allowed. Englishmen are not given to visions, certainly not in solid oak, the type of the nation; and this room would delight the heart of the true Briton. Nothing flimsy, nothing stuccoed or veneered. Oak floor, oak wainscoting, oak ceiling, tapestry paper, oil paintings, oak furniture and a table with such a solid top and well braced legs that it fairly dares one to thump on it, jump on it, to show how firm it is for the honor of old England."

DIVISION OF LABOUR

While the Macdonalds were the primary occupants and beneficiaries of the glories and conveniences of this beautiful house, there were two female servants who also lived here. The separation of their lives from the Macdonalds is clearly expressed in these floor plans. The domestics' days were spent mostly in the smaller block at the back of the house, where their bedrooms and various work rooms were located.

Their own private rooms were also inspected: "The rooms for the servants [a maid and a cook] are finished in cedar, as the rest of the house, and are large and pleasant rooms." To have mentioned the servants' quarters seems curious, yet begs the question at to how the tour might have looked from their point of view. Imagine the servants describing Dalnavert from an altogether different perspective:

"Entering through the back door, the visitor is in a large and well organized kitchen, with all the modern conveniences supplied to reduce the drudgery of the servant's life all of whom have been up since 5:30 a.m. turning on lights and the furnace, setting the table and cooking breakfast. A fully stocked pantry and larder are heavily shelved, from top to bottom, and contain all that the Macdonald family could want. We need only stand on a small stool to reach the items we need on the topmost shelf. The smells of cooking and obnoxious noises from deliveries are sensitively excluded from the main section of the house by a solid Michigan red oak door. Access to the main floor of the house, for the domestics to carry out their daily chores such as scrubbing, sweeping, tablesetting, and polishing is via a good solid cedar door that obscures and minimizes views of servants by guests. A narrow back staircase winds up to the second floor, providing the servants with discreet access to their own private rooms, their sewing rooms and bedding closets and, with the transition delicately yet authoritatively marked by a simple stair, up into the private apartments of the Macdonald family. Here, the mundane work of making and preparing beds, cleaning, scrubbing and disinfecting bathrooms, sweeping floors, polishing and dusting woodwork are carried out with discretion and modesty."

A FAMOUS SON

Sir Hugh John Macdonald (1850-1929) was the only son of Canada's first Prime Minister Sir John A. Macdonald. Sir Hugh was a lawyer by training and moved to Manitoba in 1882. He followed his father into politics, serving as a Member of Parliament and briefly as Premier of Manitoba in 1900. He was a well respected Police Magistrate and was knighted in 1913.

Margaret Laurence House

"That house in Manawaka is the one which, more than any other, I carry with me."

THAT HOUSE WAS REAL, and the renowned novelist Margaret Laurence spent more than a decade there, from the age of nine until 20 (1935-1944). And Manawaka was also real, a stand-in for Neepawa, her birthplace.

Houses figure prominently in many of her books. For example, the structural parallel between the house in *The Stone Angel* and the inflexible nature of Hagar Shipley is well known to devotees of the book. But it is in the short stories of *A Bird in the House* that the very real walls and rooms of this particular building assume life. The book opens with the sentence quoted above, and continues:

Known to the rest of the town as "the old Connor place" and to the family as the Brick House, it was plain as the winter turnips in its root cellar, sparsely windowed as some crusader's embattled fortress in a heathen wilderness, its rooms in a perpetual gloom except in the brief height of summer. Many other brick structures had existed in Manawaka for as much as half a century, but at the time when my grandfather built his house, part dwelling place and part massive monument, it had been the first of its kind.

Set back at a decent distance from the street, it was screened by a line of spruce trees whose green-black branches swept down to the earth like the sternly protective wings of giant hawks. Spruce was not indigenous in that part of the prairies. Timothy Connor had brought the seedlings all the way from Galloping Mountain, a hundred miles north, not on whim, one may be sure, but feeling that they were the trees for him. By the mid-thirties, the spruces were taller than the house, and two generations of children had clutched at boughs which were as rough and hornily knuckled as the hands of old farmers, and had swung themselves up to secret sanctuaries.

Other images and symbols illuminate *A Bird in the House,* but the Brick House, always emphatically capitalized, is ever-present, the setting for the action and deeply symbolic. It is alternately a cage, a cave, a prison, a desert: "The yard of the Brick House looked huge, a white desert, and the pale gashing streaks of light pointed up the caverns and the hollowed places where the wind had sculptured the snow."

The actual history of the house is more mundane. It was built around 1900 by her grandparents, the Simpsons. John Simpson, who figures prominently in the Manawaka novels, usually as a stiff, opinionated and humourless presence, owned a furniture store and was an undertaker, a common combination of vocations at the time. The house was a typical Victorian creation, pared down in its details to suit John Simpson, as well as to respond to the hard climate in which he lived.

Visiting the house today, which operates as the Margaret Laurence Museum, defies the ominous character suggested in her books. Certainly it is unadorned, but today the house is filled with light, and the ornate wooden details are elegant.

MARGARET LAURENCE

Margaret Laurence was an internationally renowned author, born and raised in Neepawa. After graduating in 1947 from Winnipeg's United College, she worked as a reporter with the *Winnipeg Citizen.* Her years in Africa during the 1950s inspired her first novel, *This Side Jordan* (1961), which met with critical acclaim. Neepawa provided the setting for five later novels set in the fictional prairie town of Manawaka. Vivid prairie imagery and assertion of human dignity suffuse these works. Laurence received two Governor-General's awards for fiction and became a Companion of the Order of Canada in 1971.

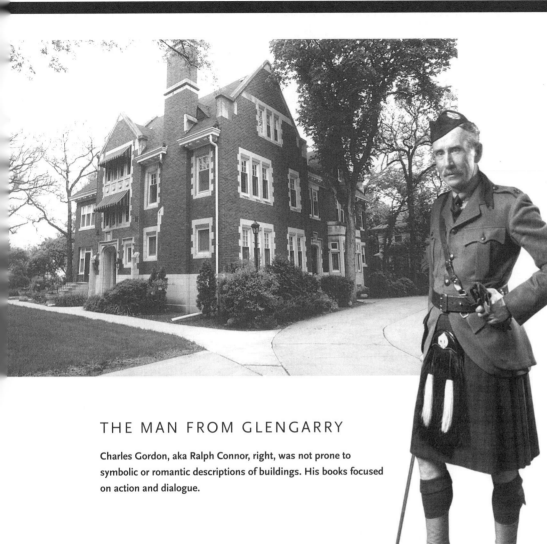

THE MAN FROM GLENGARRY

Charles Gordon, aka Ralph Connor, right, was not prone to symbolic or romantic descriptions of buildings. His books focused on action and dialogue.

Ralph Connor House

THE OWNERS OF Winnipeg's first generation of mansions were part of an economic elite, scions of wealthy eastern families and self-made millionaires who had built their fortunes in the city's burgeoning grain trade, wholesaling, industrial, manufacturing and financial sectors. They were often hard-nosed, invariably male. They were fellows concerned with the muscular world of commerce, and with the basic truths of the bottom line. The mansions they built were often like them: impressive, sturdy and implacable, monuments to their wealth, power and sophistication.

Typically their class gathered into exclusive enclaves; Armstrong's Point was for many years a prime destination. The area resonated with the names of many of the city's movers and shakers: A.G.B. Bannatyne the famous merchant, George Wood the hardware baron, Stewart Tupper son of the former Prime Minster and a renowned barrister, H.N. Ruttan the City Engineer, Joseph Dubuc the famous politician and businessman, Donald Bain the well-known wholesaler, J.B. Monk the manager of the Bank of Ottawa.

One of the most commanding mansions on the Point, at 54 Westgate, fits in comfortably, a sturdy brick and stone vision from architect George W. Northwood. Oddly, however, the home was the product of a source of unique prosperity. It was not, like so many other homes in the area, built from the profits of commerce, but instead on royalties from writing. The home of Charles W. Gordon, better known as Ralph Connor, was familiar to the many school children in the area who were required to read the books he wrote.

Charles Gordon was a major figure in Manitoba's history. He was a dedicated clergyman, who as Moderator, helped persuade Presbyterians to join in the United Church of Canada in 1925. A popular speaker, he toured Canada and the United States to raise funds for the war effort during World War I. In 1920 Gordon was appointed by the federal government to chair the Joint Council of Industry, a labour negotiation board. His pseudonym, Ralph Connor, was better known, however, as a best-selling Canadian author. His literary skills brought him the fame and fortune that allowed him to build his handsome Armstrong Point home.

Gordon slapped down $50,000 in 1913-14 for this house, the equivalent of $800,000 in 2000. It was a suitable expression of the riches and accomplishments of one Ralph Connor, famous novelist. Conversely, it is difficult to gauge just how comfortable the devout Presbyterian clergyman Charles Gordon felt about the ostentatious show of worldly wealth and material possessions of his alter-ego.

WOMEN TO THE RESCUE

When Gordon died in 1937 the family found itself in serious trouble. There were back taxes owing on 54 Westgate and the City of Winnipeg, which had contemplated demolishing it, was relieved when the University Women's Club stepped forward to rent the facility. Chartered in 1909, the Club was active in various social causes. After years of meeting in rented rooms it was a big step for the Club to rent an entire house, but within six years the gamble had paid off. Membership tripled and in 1945 they bought Gordon's former home and undertook minor renovations. The original character of the house remains as it was in 1914.

Ambassador Apartments

PARTS OF WINNIPEG'S HEART are a tangle of streets, giving the city a bit of old-world European charm. That tangle is the result of an ancient system of land division and ownership. The pattern, identified by its relationship to waterways, was known as the river lot system. The principal characteristic of the system involved the creation of long narrow strips of land that stretched back from the Red and Assiniboine rivers, providing each lot with its own river frontage, giving access to water for drinking and washing but also for transportation.

Because the rivers take impressively winding courses, it was common for river lots to intersect at irregular angles. As the City of Winnipeg grew in the late 19th century, those intersections often had important implications for traffic patterns, as the river lots formed the basis for many streets. The most dramatic angles occurred where Portage Avenue, Main Street and Notre Dame Avenue, and the thoroughfares parallel to them, met.

Nearly every building in downtown Winnipeg still readily conforms to the standard rectangle in their floor plans, without regard for the occasionally awkward intersections. But some don't. The Ambassador Apartments is one such building.

With its two main faces running along Hargrave Street and Cumberland Avenue, the building is in plan a sharp-edged triangle. It's one of just a handful of buildings whose shape still dramatically embraces the old river lot divisions that characterized the farming landscape of the early 1900s.

The Ambassador is also an important reminder of Winnipeg's love affair with the apartment building, particularly before World War I. The city took to the concept like no other place in Canada. By 1911 there were about 100 apartment buildings in the city, ten times the number of blocks elsewhere, including Montreal and Toronto. Buildings like the Ambassador, with its impressive architecture, were sure signs of the importance placed on these new additions to Winnipeg's housing stock.

The Ambassador Apartments was built in 1909 for entrepreneurs John McArthur and James Fisher, and was originally named the Breadalbane. Architect John Woodman created an impressive building, exploiting the triangular lot to create a dramatic corner signature for the building. The powerfully composed entrance on Hargrave Street, with its cantilevered canopy, double-return staircase and carved stone balusters, hinted at the elegance within.

RIVER LOTS

This detail of an old aerial view of Winnipeg shows the property lines of the historic river lot system, now expressed as streets.

Eaton House

This exquisite mansion is firmly associated with its second owners, Gilbert and Marjorie Eaton, members at one time of a sort of Canadian royalty, the famous Eaton's department store family. In his design, Winnipeg architect Arthur Cubbidge looked to the stately and rugged character of the late Gothic Revival style, particularly French Norman and English Tudor, for this expression of high architectural sophistication. The placement of each brick was so important to the building's character that Cubbidge spent a good deal of time in 1932, on-site. instructing the bricklayers in the techniques required, and the brick placements demanded.

THE RED AND ASSINIBOINE rivers were, at the opening of the 19th century, the necessary focus for settlement. They were critical sources for basic survival, providing water, fish and transportation to those crowded along their banks. By the late 19th century, however, river banks were increasingly sought-after by the wealthy. Mansions went up along the Assiniboine, on both the south and north shores, west of the confluence of the two rivers. Broadway, Assiniboine Avenue and Roslyn Road became the sites for massive mansions and gorgeous grounds. Further west of these concentrations of wealth, several well known high-end developments were created. Armstrong's Point, Crescentwood, Wellington Crescent and Tuxedo, all along or at least near the Assiniboine River, were studded with the city's largest and finest houses, with spacious, groomed grounds.

It is Wellington Crescent that has become embedded as Winnipeg's "mile of luxury." Visitors glide along its gently winding and heavily treed route and the stately mansions of local aristocracy are pointed to with pride and awe. No house is the object of more interest than the former Eaton House. Built in 1932, and originally the home of James Gilchrist, Vice President of Searle Grain, it is more firmly associated with its next owners Gilbert and Marjorie Eaton, members of the famous Eaton's department store family. This remarkable building is an exceptional example of French Norman Gothic architecture, the style choice for many homes of the wealthy in the 1920s and 1930s.

WELLINGTON CRESCENT

Today, it is the western half of Wellington Crescent that is best known to Winnipeggers for its expensive mansions. But the actual development of the western section of the Crescent was not begun until the 1920s. This image shows the original eastern part, near St. Mary's Academy.

Lost Treasures — Houses

Given the vagaries of time, and of fashion, it is not surprising that over the years Manitoba has lost hundreds of fine houses. This collage suggests the great range of homes that have been lost and ways of life lost with them.

The area now known as Osborne Village in Winnipeg, was once home to dozens of Manitoba's wealthiest citizens. Roslyn Road was the epicentre of wealth, with great mansions on splendid grounds lined up along its length. On the east side of Osborne Street, on the river side, there once sat side by side two houses of unbelievable grandeur. **The Sutherland House** (right) and **the Ross House** (bottom) fell victim, like so many others nearby, of their size and of the economics of urbanization. Simply, they were too big to be sustained, and the land on which they sat too valuable. They were torn down to make way for apartment blocks.

The D.H. Mc Fadden House in Emerson, from around the 1900, was lost several years ago.

RESIDENCE OF HON A.G.B.BANNATYNE.

Winnipeg once had a splendid collection of terrace houses. This example on Edmonton Street, between St. Mary and Graham, was a popular residential choice for many middle class families from about 1880 to 1910. As the city's downtown core gave way to commercial ventures and more cost-efficient apartment buildings, the terraces came down.

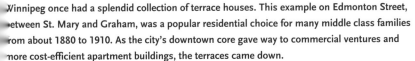

In the 1880s, two fabulous homes were immediately upheld by Winnipeggers as examples of the city's wealth and sophistication. One was **the Bannatyne House** (above) on what would become Armstrong's Point. The other was the so-called **Pile of Bones Villa** on James Avenue, a creation of early Winnipeg architects Barber and Barber. Both buildings succumbed long, long ago.

Chapter 2

FARMS

Sandison Farm

IT HAS SEEN BETTER DAYS. Still, the Sandison farm, just north of Brandon, claims one of the most fantastic tales of the late 1800s. The farm serves as the backdrop for a classical tale featuring the central character, John Sandison. It's a rags to riches, then back again to rags plotline, and the house John Sandison built in 1892 is a vital ingredient of the story.

Sandison was a Scottish immigrant who arrived in the Carberry Plains region, east of Brandon, in 1884. His skill as a farmhand was acknowledged for three consecutive years, when he captured first-place honours at the Carberry plowing matches. However, Sandison's ambitions exceeded simply being an exemplary farm labourer.

In 1886 he and his new wife Elizabeth bought a section of land six kilometres north of Brandon, where they commenced upon a typical hard-scrabble pioneer lifestyle. They lived in a log shanty, roofed with sod. Their first crop was broadcast by hand. Within a year, however, John Sandison's story rose beyond the mere typical to the near mythical.

For the next seven years, Sandison's ardent ambition and venturesome daring made him one of the province's foremost farmers. He embarked on a program of land acquisition and cultivation that saw his original 160 hectares increase to 1120 hectares by 1890. Local newspapers referred to him as "Our Bonanza Farmer" and the "Wheat King," nor were these idle appellations. He owned large farms near Souris and Kemnay, brought Scottish farm labourers to the Brandon area to work his massive estates, and built up a virtual agricultural arsenal of farming machinery and implements. Sandison was even featured in colonization materials prepared by the Canadian Pacific Railway as an exemplar of all that could be accomplished in the uncultivated West by dint of hard labour.

With his farming operations securely under way, Sandison turned his attention to creating a fitting monument to his success.

Sandison House is one of the grandest farm houses in Manitoba. Constructed from exquisite granite fieldstone, the building boasts features and details—a look-out tower, chimney pots, date-stone shield, bell—not found on any other Manitoba farm house. During its construction it was reported that Sandison found the placement and colour of one of the stones so objectionable to his personal aesthetic that he forced the stonemasons to tear a salient in the wall to replace it.

WHEAT KING

In just seven years John Sandison grew one of Manitoba's largest farming operations. Here, seen posing on horseback in the early 1890s, in front of a selection of his binders, he was every inch the Scottish lord, although his background suggested more humble roots. Lionized by the western press, Sandison came to epitomize the great opportunities available in Canada's West. He had arrived here with very little, and made his fortune with a mix of hard labour, perseverance and shrewd calculations. The final episode of the story—his downfall—seems to have been of little interest to those who extolled his many successes. Sandison went out like a lamb, leaving behind an unglamorous final chapter full of failure and insolvency for his aggrandizing supporters to mull over.

A WHOPPING GOOD YARN

John Sandison's larger-than-life story aroused in some the need for a dramatic conclusion. The most entertaining story (which cannot be confirmed), was compiled by J.T. McGregor, and featured diamonds, mysterious late night rendezvous and Scotland Yard detectives. According to McGregor's account, Sandison fled Canada one evening late in May of 1893, just one step ahead of the law. Rumour had it that he had spent the winter in Scotland, buying up diamonds on credit to pay off his Canadian creditors. After returning to Canada, a Scotland Yard detective was reportedly sent to track him down and to bring the scoundrel Sandison back to justice. After checking in at the Grand Union Hotel in Brandon, the detective, a "middle-aged, slightly greying Englishman" struck up a conversation with the proprietor, a friend of the Sandisons who suspected the newcomer was on the trail for Sandison.

With his new guest safely ensconced in the hotel, the proprietor rode out to the Sandisons at midnight to tip off John. Brandon's Wheat King was reported to have loaded up two bags and to have made a mad dash for the passenger train due at a whistle stop east of Brandon. When Elizabeth Sandison awoke the next morning she found her husband had disappeared. Some reports had him turning up in Argentina, married to a wealthy widow. Others claimed that he was seen in South Africa, mining diamonds.

In 1892 he commissioned Brandon architect W.R. Marshall to design what would become one of Manitoba's finest farm houses. The result was a veritable baronial Scottish manor, grand and tough, with a delicate wrap-around verandah and whimsical lookout tower. The interior was lavishly appointed with oak panelling and decorative plasterwork. A demanding client, Sandison's numerous changes and revisions dragged construction well into 1893. The delays meant that neither he, nor Elizabeth, would ever enjoy a single night in the house, for circumstances were about to change, for the worse, for the Wheat King.

As early as 1891 Sandison's grand schemes were beginning to unravel. That year a frost levied severe damage to his crops, and although he rebounded the following year, he was deeply in debt. Instead of cutting back production, however, in 1893 he gambled on an even greater yield, borrowing heavily to finance new machinery and seed. His creditors had reportedly been watching his huge operation closely and by May were having doubts about Sandison's plans and his ability to repay his monumental debt. Before the autumn harvest of that year the farm was seized.

Then Sandison vanished. He seems to have abandoned the country, for his name disappears from local newspapers. As for Elizabeth, reports suggest that she returned to her father's farm near Carberry, herself disappearing into the mists of the past.

BARN RAISING

Ontario farming traditions, transplanted to Manitoba with the arrival in the late 19th century of thousands of Anglo-Ontario immigrants, required a large barn to hold livestock and the necessary straw, hay and grain for their maintenance. In many cases these barns were built into a hill so that a farmer could drive into the loft at the higher level, or into the stable at the lower level. The great barn that once stood on the Sandison farm is now gone, but the stone foundation walls trace its position. This photograph, showing the construction of a typical Ontario-style barn, suggests the likely character of Sandison's building.

Bohémier Farm

IN 1870, WHEN MANITOBA ENTERED CONFEDERATION, the province was a rich tableaux of cultures with two main linguistic groups dominating. The census undertaken that year confirmed that fact. Of a total population of about 15,000, half spoke French, the other half English.

The French-speaking segment of the population, consisting of both native-born Métis and immigrants from Quebec, had fought hard to protect their language, education and land ownership rights in the Manitoba Act. They must have looked on with mounting alarm during the 1870s and '80s as both federal and provincial government immigration policies resulted in the arrival of more and more English-speaking immigrants into the province.

As early as the 1870s, in the face of the English-speaking immigrant onslaught, Métis were selling their land and moving further west to what would become Saskatchewan. Franco-Manitobans originally from Quebec stood their ground. During the 1880s Bishop Alexandre-Antonin Taché of St. Boniface, and the French-speaking lay leadership, took practical steps to stem the tide of English land colonization. They purchased blocks of formerly-owned Métis land and invited French Canadians from Quebec and New England to settle here. Their efforts were only moderately successful, however, and by the time of the 1901 census French-speaking Manitobans numbered only 6% of the total population of 255,211.

What they had lost in numbers, they made up for in grit and determination. Language, literature and drama were the primary tools in ongoing efforts to preserve their French-language culture. Architecture also proved to be a powerful visual connection to their heritage. Other settlement groups happily replaced their "national" vernacular architecture—the centuries-old traditional folk designs and construction techniques that described their origins—within a decade in favour of prevailing North American architectural tastes. Many Franco-Manitoba pioneers, however, continued to build using the potent domestic architectural traditions of Quebec and France, and so it was with Benjamin Bohémier.

Bohémier, (1848-1926), a lumber merchant from Ste-Anne-des-Plaines, Quebec, arrived in Manitoba in 1883 and in 1889 built a farm house south of Winnipeg, in the Parish of St. Norbert. The house, though modest in size, was a strong model of contemporary French architecture. Its distinctive roof shape and elegant details stood as an expressive beacon on the Manitoba prairies for a culture that would not be ignored.

PRETTY BIG

By today's standards the Bohémier family was large, with eight children. But at the turn of the century, when it was not uncommon for farm families to boast at least a dozen youngsters, the Bohémiers were just typical.

THE FRENCH BARN, DISTINCTLY PURE

Unlike other settlement groups, those of French heritage conceived farm buildings as separate units housing distinct functions. Thus, the Mennonite concept of combining a house and a barn in a single building was not embraced, nor was the English tradition of uniting hay storage with livestock in a single structure. On a Franco-Manitoban farm one would typically find a barn for hay, a barn for horses and a barn for cattle. Where their houses exhibited great architectural flare, in their barn designs Franco-Manitobans chose a look that was, simply put, plain.

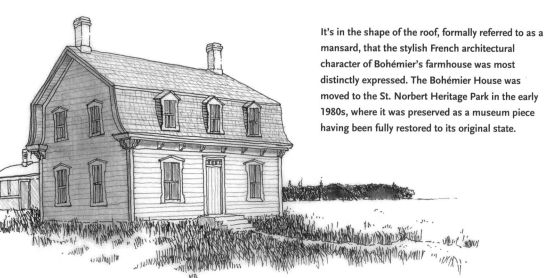

It's in the shape of the roof, formally referred to as a mansard, that the stylish French architectural character of Bohémier's farmhouse was most distinctly expressed. The Bohémier House was moved to the St. Norbert Heritage Park in the early 1980s, where it was preserved as a museum piece having been fully restored to its original state.

The Johnson House sits less than 50 metres from the shore of Lake Winnipeg. The face of the building stares happily out onto a product of commerce—fish—and defiantly onto the possibility of death – the deceptively placid-looking shallow waters of Lake Winnipeg.

Johnson House

ALL BUILDINGS ARE FORCED TO RESPOND TO climate, their shapes and outer patina verifying the response they proffer. Roofs, their first line of defense against the ravages of wind, rain and snow, are especially evocative of their response. Often steeply pitched, they are ripe with possibilities for sculptural expression. We are so familiar with the strong triangular shapes, however, that we do not usually register roofs as either interesting or memorable. On Hecla Island, nestled just off the west shore of Lake Winnipeg, about 160 kilometres north of Winnipeg, there exists a collection of little buildings which defy indifference. Icelandic pioneers who settled on Hecla Island in the late 1800s constructed homes with roof shapes that dramatically describe the presence of the wind, as well as recalling the maritime origins of their indigenous culture.

The Johnson House is the best preserved of the bunch. This tiny building is a study into how basic, familiar forms can be skewed slightly, taking on new, even powerful architectural and design character. Seen from a distance, it is the structure's roof that commands attention. The typical gable roof form, seen on so many houses, is strikingly stretched backward so that its sleek aerodynamic shape conjures up a sense of the strong westerly winds blowing over it. It's as if the force of the wind has elongated the roof. Recalling images of Icelandic maritime history, one can also imagine the roof as the hull of a boat, upturned and placed snugly atop the building.

MURALS

The walls of many early Icelandic homes were decorated with mural paintings, often applied directly onto the walls. The predominant subject of these paintings was the Icelandic landscape, rugged and beautiful. Human habitation was typically conveyed through the presence of farm buildings, as seen here. A review of historical Icelandic images and old photographs suggests that a building like the Johnson House, and the others like it on Hecla Island, had no precedent in Iceland. The designs on Hecla Island were the result of local Icelandic genius.

BOAT AS ROOF?

This small dory floating off Hecla Island in the 1940s may be one of the sources for inspiration for the roof shape of the Johnson House.

Mennonite Housebarn

IN THE COUNTRYSIDE southeast of Morden and Winkler, about an hour south of Winnipeg, the remnants of early Mennonite settlements lie dotted in places with names such as Neubergthal, Reinland, Chortitz, Schowenweise, Gnadenthal.

Mennonite immigrants who arrived in Manitoba, beginning in 1876, brought very distinct settlement and building traditions to their new land. The settlement pattern was based on an ancient land-holding system that featured a so-called "strip village," surrounded by an arrangement of long narrow fields called koagels allotted equally to farmers according to quality and location. Within the system, buildings took on a special configuration: firstly, they were lined up in a neat row facing the street, and secondly the two major buildings on each site—the house and the barn—were combined in one long, continuous form.

The origins of the strip village, and of the housebarn, can be traced to Dutch and Russian influences. In the Netherlands, where many Manitoba Mennonites trace their origins, the combination of a house and a barn was a familiar development, conveniently combining work and leisure, allowing the family to tend to farm duties under cover. Even the farming village street was familiar in Europe.

For Mennonites, however, there were more immediate reasons to adopt such an arrangement. In Russia, where Mennonite settlers had been invited by Empress Catherine the Great to establish settlements in the 18th century, villages prospered, but were under constant threat of attack from the local Tatar population. A compact, easily defensible arrangement, the strip village was a perfect solution.

Subsequently the strip village came to symbolize important aspects of Mennonite culture, like a communal spirit, a profound sense of social cohesiveness and, as expressed through their designs, an appreciation for simplicity and conformity. This design conformity, in true communal fashion, also prevented social stratification based on the show of personal wealth.

The building configuration was practical, characterized by long, narrow lots. This layout ensured efficiency. A person could easily get to the barn in a matter of steps and without facing the inclemencies of the harsh Manitoba weather. Additionally, warmth was generated from the farm animals and hay which was located in close proximity.

Amazingly, dozens of these traditional Mennonite housebarns still stand, and many are even used as they were a hundred years ago. Typically, they are now occupied by the descendants of Altkolonier (Old School) Mennonites returning from Mexico, where about 3,200 had gone in 1919 to avoid interference from the Manitoba government in their language and education rights.

A traditional Mennonite village, with its line of housebarns, was usually focused on a windmill to grind the communities grain.

TIMELESS BEAUTY

This scene bears a resemblance to an Old Masters painting. A carefully composed group looks on, apparently at nothing in particular, for there is no obvious focal point. Their expressions evoke an ethereal sense of dignity; they seem unshakable in their repose as they are seemingly lost in thought. A viewer might wonder, "Why did they gather together? What were they thinking about? Why are they so calm?" Actually, this is no painting. It is a photograph from around 1955 of a Manitoba Mennonite household. Dramatically offset by a back-drop of richly patterned and vibrant wallpaper, these Mennonites reflect the practicality and tranquility that defines their religious and cultural beliefs.

THE GLORIES OF WOOD

Mennonites, like American Shakers (an offshoot of the Quakers), whose simple furniture is now highly sought after by collectors, were attentive to the smallest details of their buildings. They mastered the properties of materials, particularly wood, and understood how to effectively assemble things. While their design rejected big, flamboyant statements, they found their own unique forms of expression. Mennonite culture, like their designs, has for centuries taken delight in rendering the workaday into something of casual, yet spectacular beauty. Crafts, like intricate paper cutting and modest wooden sculptures, were popular practices. Illuminated manuscripts, executed with superb penmanship were also highly respected.

Playful, stylish profiles or curves cannot be found on Mennonite housebarns or farm buildings. However, almost any door leading into a barn or a granary was highlighted with a pattern of criss-crossing wooden strips that created a richly textured and inviting surface. The various joints connecting log or timber sections also were assessed for aesthetic possibilities, as is the case of typical beam-brace-post connections in barns, right.

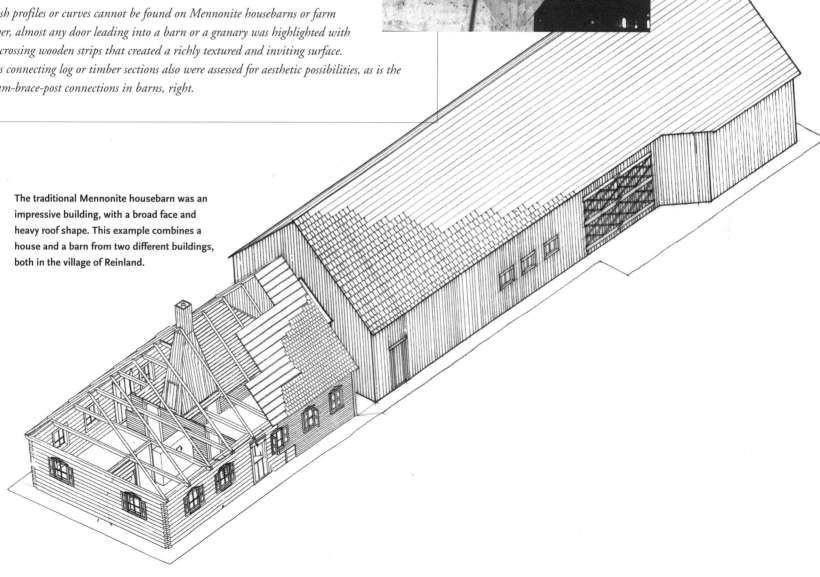

The traditional Mennonite housebarn was an impressive building, with a broad face and heavy roof shape. This example combines a house and a barn from two different buildings, both in the village of Reinland.

Christina Guild House

CHRISTINA GUILD was a bright young woman, no different than many other bright young women living in Manitoba at the turn of the century.

She was born at Kemnay, near Brandon, in 1891, the daughter of William Guild and his wife Anna, and the solitary sister to four brothers. By the time she was a teenager she had become keenly interested in farm issues and studied Home Economics at the University of Manitoba. She was deeply involved in the local Manitoba Women's Institute, a province-wide organization that sought solutions to deal with pioneer women's problems and needs.

None of these pursuits made Christina Guild special. Many women followed a similar path as they undertook to make a difference in their communities. What did make Christina Guild different in 1916 was her involvement in the field of architecture.

By the turn of the 20th century many issues associated specifically with women were becoming the source for concern and debate. Suffrage (the right to vote) was the defining issue, but there were many others, like prohibition, property rights and education. As part of this final area, activists and educators began to look at farm houses for improvement. And who better to consult than the women who actually lived and worked in them. Thus in May of 1916, through advertisements in various magazines, the Manitoba Agricultural College in Winnipeg solicited applications from farm women to provide "the best ideas in farm house planning."

Christina Guild was one of 63 women who entered the "Better Farm Homes Competition," one of six who won a prize, and the only one whose design was actually built and still survives.

All six winning schemes were gathered together in a booklet (put out in 1917 by the provincial Department of Agriculture and Immigration) and distributed throughout the province. And 34 sets of plans were also sold by the College. Which designs were chosen is not known, nor are the results of their use.

Christina's ideas were used. Her father built the family house relying entirely on his daughter's plans, and also followed much of the exterior designs provided in the final rendered image (that is, window placement and size). The one obvious difference is in the roof. Where the perspective drawing had featured a steep pyramidal form, the Guilds relied on the more familiar (and in Manitoba, practical) shallow hip-shape with projecting dormer windows.

The actual process that brought Christian Guild's, and the other four women's, winning ideas to fruition is not known in its details. None of the women's original plan drawings, which were to form the basis for their entries have survived. It is known that Francis Parr, a Winnipeg architect and A.S. Corrigill, an architecture student, worked the women's sketches and ideas up into technical drawings and perspectives. It's interesting that these men invariably placed the farm houses not into a rural context but into a romantic and quasi-urban context – with things like sidewalks and carefully groomed parks.

Christina Guild's father altered the roof shape to create a more familiar shallow pyramidal form.

A BUREAUCRAT IN THE KITCHEN

While contestants were expected to deal with all aspects of floor planning, it was the kitchen that became the real focus for attention. In the provincial government's Extension Bulletin *that announced the winners, it was the description of the kitchen that invariably took up the most space. And for each set of plans, a more detailed drawing of the kitchen was also supplied. For example, for Christina Guild's house, the judges (L.J. Smith, Professor of Agricultural Engineering; Margaret Kennedy, Professor of Household Art (both faculty at the Agricultural College) and Mrs. M.E. McBeath a well known pioneer woman from Headingley) wrote:*

The kitchen has but one outside wall; but with the arrangement of doors, there should be no difficulty in securing ample ventilation in warm weather. The pantry is located conveniently between the kitchen and dining room. In the corner is a clothes chute leading down from the bathroom. The chute does not detract from the pantry, since the space that it occupies would be hard to utilize, being in the corner between shelves on the left and the little table-cupboard under the window at the right. Many would put a slide in the partition between the pantry and the dining room.

This fascinating array of gadgets and appliances was intended to lighten the load of housewives at the turn of the century. Clockwise from top left: a folding wash tub stand; the "Chief Rapid Hand Corn Sheller;" a clothes washer, this one called "The Canadian," offered by Eaton's; the "Royal Alexandra" Stove, also offered by Eaton's; the "Leonard Cleanable Refrigerator;" and "Maid-Rite Silver" washboard.

Bender Hamlet

BENDER HAMLET IS A DESOLATE SPOT. How could anyone have lived here? The hamlet is full of stones. How could anyone have farmed here? But oddly enough people did live here, and farmed. For a time they even prospered. This valiant attempt at farming in rugged terrain was one of only two Jewish farm settlements attempted in Manitoba.

Bender Hamlet was the more substantial of the two, but it didn't last long. Just 24 years, from 1903 to 1927. Its existence, however, is a testament to a sturdy pioneer spirit.

The history of the site begins in the dreams of Jacob Bender, a farmer from Nikolaiev in Russian Ukraine, who persuaded friends to journey with him to Canada. The Canadian government granted the group a quarter section of land (NE 36-19-1W) for their village site, which was divided by the group into 20 lots, each approximately 43 metres wide. Nineteen houses were quickly erected, arranged side-by-side in a long row as if on an urban street, similar to Mennonite strip villages that still exist in south-central Manitoba (see page 32). That similarity is not surprising since the two groups came from the same area and would have shared similar farming techniques.

The strip village was an efficient, and traditional solution for close-knit farming communities, allowing easy access from the single road to every house in the community. At Bender Hamlet the Jewish settlers built a school and synagogue. The community had a full-time Cantor, Schochet (Kosher butcher), Mohel (circumcisor) and a Rabbi who visited from Winnipeg, and lived according to the tenets of the Orthodox Jewish faith.

Given the nature of this land—part of a massive gravel deposit—farming proved to be a constant struggle. Cereal grain farming was impossible, and although cattle farming proved profitable for several years, the collapse after World War I of cattle prices left the colony in dire straits. Appeals were made to the Jewish Colonization Association for assistance. And although they received $500, and were thus inspired to rename their community Narcisse to honour Narcisse Levin, president of the Association, it was not possible to continue. By 1927 the last family had abandoned the colony and the buildings were dismantled. The site and especially the cemetery are still well-maintained by descendants, but all that's left of the community are the faint signs of a trail and a few low mounds that mark building sites.

Little is known about the individual buildings at Bender Hamlet. In terms of architectural character, the homes are modest, and comfortingly similar, giving the village a coherent, attractive appearance. There must have been barns and outbuildings at Bender Hamlet but none of these are visible here. This fact marks a significant distinction between this strip village and the Mennonite strip villages which they superficially resemble, in which homes and barns were connected.

This tower, just east of Stonewall, is one of a handful of farm buildings left to recall a once vibrant industry which reached its heyday in the 1930s – fur farming.

A BRUTAL BUSINESS

"Foxes are killed by crushing the chest walls. They are placed on their sides, and the slaughterer places the soles of his feet immediately behind the foreleg and bears down with his full weight. They are also killed by forcing the head back until the neck breaks. The information available indicates that the adoption of some more humane method of killing, such as the use of chloroform or ether, would not injure the fur and, at the same time, be more merciful." From Fur-Farming in Canada, J. Walter Jones, 1914.

Fox Farm Tower

BROAD FIELDS OF WHEAT, OATS, BARLEY, alfalfa and canola give southern Manitoba its beautiful carpet of summer colours—yellow, gold, violet. Southern Manitoba is farming country. The region also boasts a long history of animal farming, with large operations devoted to cattle, chickens and hogs. The buildings best associated with these endeavours are well known to Manitobans—stately barns, silver granaries, quonset huts, long low chicken coops. A less familiar, tall, lean tower-like building recalls another and lesser-known aspect of Manitoba's agricultural history—fur farming.

There were once dozens of fur-farming operations in Manitoba, scattered throughout the south. Primary subjects for farming were foxes and minks, but raccoons, fishers, beavers, muskrats, otters, martens and even skunks were occasionally raised for their pelts. At the fur farming industry's height, in the 1930s and 40s, more than 25,000 pelts per year were sent from Manitoba farms to fur markets in Toronto and London, and the province often ranked in the top five producers of furs in Canada.

The tower was the most emblematic structure of a fur farming business. At its base were spread scores of animal pens, often of rudimentary construction—posts strung together with diamond-shaped wire—with the purpose of firmly keeping the animals in place. The fur farm incorporated simple breeding and monetary concepts: let a highly prized male sire mate with female vixens to produce the season's "crop" of pups whose furs would become the source of wealth.

The tower was vital in ensuring a successful crop. It provided the altitude necessary for a farmer to view the animals during the so-called whelping season, the most critical period in the fur farm calendar. It was at this time, usually in February, that foxes and minks mated, and produced the pups whose furs would be ready for harvest by the following winter, when they were their thickest and most luxuriant.

In order to produce the largest crop possible, it was essential to separate the male sire from a female vixen. This was accomplished, practically, by the farmer in the tower shouting directions down to his assistants. The sire then would be whisked around by the assistants from female to female. This was carried out with great care to avoid any disruption to the animals which, still wild, tended to be exceptionally jittery at this time.

It was from the tower that a keen eye was also kept on the new mothers, which, if agitated might kill their pups. In Prince Edward Island, the site of the most fur farms in Canada at the time, local laws forbade people from approaching a fur farm in the whelping season.

Negrycz Farm

A SMALL RIVER GENTLY WINDS ITS WAY through a scant birch wood. Hills bend and curve upward from the flow to a level tract draped in the thick greens of summer prairie grass. The sky above seems to seal you in this place, while a soothing breeze wanders by. The birch leaves sigh. In this place, there is natural perfection. Life as it should be – unspoiled. The calm is pronounced, pure and original. The place? The Negrycz Farm.

Ukrainian immigrants arriving in Manitoba in the late 19th century were often forced to the very edges of known settlement. The Parkland region was a prime destination. Their early years were hard; still they persevered, even flourished.

Remnants of the early years—small log houses and barns featuring thatched roofs—are now few and far between. Remarkably, however, there remains a single complete set of original log farm buildings in the Parkland area known as the Negrycz Farm. The farm is the best-preserved pioneer Ukrainian farm site in Manitoba with some buildings dating from 1897. The home feels completely isolated from the outer world as it is setback off the highway and completely surrounded by trees.

Siblings Anna and Steve Negrych (the Negrycz name was anglicized shortly after their arrival in Canada), lived here, without benefit of most modern conveniences until their deaths in the 1990s. They were the last two surviving siblings of the 13 children born to Wasyl and Anna, who broke the land and built the family farm. Steve was somewhat more attached to modern life, having taught school in Dauphin for many years. Anna, however, lived almost all of her long life in the main house and toiled daily on the immaculately maintained farmsite.

The Negrycz Farm contains eleven buildings, all focused on a fenced garden and orchard.

GRASS, TWIGS, LOGS, PEGS, PLANKS, AND MUD ARCHITECTURE

The bunkhouse was in many ways a typical pioneer Ukrainian farm house, constructed of spruce and tamarack logs joined at the corners with saddlenotch joints. The bunkhouse walls were coated with mud and clay to fill in the cracks. A rough wooden door provided access. Measuring a mere 4.5 by 5.5 metres, this structure provided sleeping accommodation at the height of its use in the 1920s for seven men and boys.

This photograph illustrates two features unique to remaining Ukrainian folk buildings in Manitoba: long roof shingles and an apparently careless stack of lumber leaning against the roof. The shingles are a direct link to Ukraine, where this type of roof covering was commonly used in the Carpathian Mountains. The stack of lumber—which in fact is a very deliberate feature—funnels smoke discharged from the oven inside the building up into the attic, where it was used to cure meats which were hung there.

While logs created a sturdy enough wall, structurally, the rough surface was not what most people had in mind for a finished appearance. It was a common practice to cover the logs with a whole assemblage—plaster, mud, dung, all held in place with twigs attached to the walls—that was then painted white. Of course these materials are susceptible to deterioration, and almost every spring it was necessary to take a few days to "re-mud" and repaint.

The bunkhouse is not only a fascinating example of ancient building technologies it also houses a now-rare example of a traditional oven, in Ukrainian called a "peech." The peech was a remarkable piece of engineering and construction. Inside, it featured a framework of logs and branches covered with layers of mud, straw and clay. The resulting dramatic sculptural shape was focused on the hood section, which drew smoke from the oven and lead it outside and up to the attic where it was used to cure meats. A broad hearth encircled the main structure, providing a place to cool breads removed from the oven. But the peech was not just a cooking device. In the winter, the latent heat was exploited by the boys who slept sprawled on top.

Chapter 3

3

OFFICIAL

Prince of Wales's Fort

THE IMPOSING STAR-SHAPED STONE FORT near Churchill is a curious remnant of geopolitical maneuvering and theories of warfare that characterized relations between France and England in the 18th century.

Throughout the 1700s, England and France were engaged in a see-saw struggle for domination of sea routes and control of trade. Despite the signing of various treaties, the most important being the 1713 Treaty of Utrecht—one of whose provisions saw France cede control to England of the entire drainage basin of Hudson Bay—there were still persistent fears throughout the English realm of French attacks.

In this prickly and dangerous atmosphere, England, and many of its major corporate interests, devoted huge sums of money to creating a system of massive stone forts throughout its colonial possessions. A particularly strategic point in North America was on Hudson Bay, near the mouth of the Churchill River, a critical port in the Hudson's Bay Company fur trade operation. In 1732 the Company began construction of a major stone fortification on a peninsula opposite the present site of Churchill.

Prince of Wales's Fort was typical of 18th-century fortification design. The star-shaped walls ironically were based on the theories of a Frenchman, Sébastien Vauban. Vauban, King Louis XIV's military siege engineer in the late 1600s, designed forts with massive stone walls set on mammoth earthworks. Vauban considered the increasingly destructive power of artillery in his designs and devised star-shaped walls whose steeply-angled surfaces could more easily deflect cannon fire.

When it was completed, the walls of the Churchill fort were 12 metres thick and bristled with 40 cannon. It was certainly an impressive, and presumably intimidating presence on the coast. But when the French finally did arrive, in 1782, in the form of three ships and 400 men under the command of the Comte de la Pérouse, the vastly out-numbered English garrison turned over the place without a fight. And in a typical diplomatic exchange of the era, within a few years the fort was returned to the English.

Built over the course of 50 years, beginning in 1731, Prince of Wales's Fort near Churchill is the oldest building in Manitoba. The fort, restored by Parks Canada, is now a National Historic Site.

THE WAGES OF BATTLE

In case of attack, HBC employees at the fort were advised of the following compensation package, taken directly, with contemporary spelling, from a 1744 document:

To the Widow, Children, Father, or Mother of any Man that Shall loose his life in the defence of the Factory Thirty Pounds

To every one of them that shall loose a Leg or Arm or both in such defence Thirty Pounds.

To every one that shall receive any other wound or shall prevent any wilfull or Malicious damage to any part of the Comapnys Effects, etc., such Sum of mony as the Governor and Committee shall think fit, etc.

That every person So wounded in defense of the Factory shall be cured at the Charge of the Company.

A BRIEF HISTORY OF MANITOBA FORTS

Prince of Wales's Fort was an exceptional building in Manitoba's fur trade and military history. The stone fur trade forts on the Red River—Upper Fort Garry in present-day Winnipeg and Lower Fort Garry near present-day Selkirk— were more indicative of the type of big defensive structures the Hudson's Bay Company built. More typical was a small and simple palisaded enclosure like Brandon House, left, a Hudson's Bay Company fur trade post from the late 1700s situated south of present-day Brandon.

Vaughan Street Jail

As designed by Walter Chesterton, in 1881, the Eastern Judicial District Jail featured decorative elements that belied its function. Instead of conveying a sense of foreboding, the jail appeared elegant and inviting. Only the bars on the windows suggested what went on inside.

TODAY, ONE OF THE MOST NOTORIOUS BUILDINGS from Manitoba's past is almost invisible, sitting at an awkward bend on York Avenue in Winnipeg, obscured by the intersections of one-way streets. The Vaughan Street Jail offers an important, sometimes gruesome, glimpse into the early days of Manitoba's legal system.

When it was built, in 1881-83, the jail was part of a whole block that had been assembled as a judicial reserve. Of the three main buildings originally constructed here, during the 1880s—a Legislative Building, a Court House, and the Eastern Judicial District Jail—only the jail remains.

When it was built, the new jail was considered top of the line, a great improvement over the primitive facility used previously, a basement where inmates were imprisoned in poorly lit, low-ceilinged rooms with heavy wooden doors. The new jail had all the latest conveniences for its highly specialized function. New steel cells from P&J Pauley Bros. of St. Louis Missouri were a highlight.

The jail housed every kind of miscreant. The east wing was reserved for offenders "of the lighter stripe." The west wing was for more serious cases. And mental patients were also confined here, secured by metal staples driven into the floor. At the time, the jail was seen as "humane," but one observer still described it as being "enwrapped in Stygian gloom."

In an era that still relied on the death penalty as the absolute punishment, it was here that those sentenced to death met their fate. The condemned were marched to an exercise yard at the back of the jail where the hastily constructed gallows waited. There's no evidence of those horrors now but it's still possible, as you walk up Vaughan Street, to imagine the terror and resignation of those awaiting their date with death those many years ago.

THE PATH TO DEATH

There have been 600 people put to death in Canada since 1870. All of the condemned have taken their final breaths at the end of a rope and according to reports some of the executions were badly botched. As the Manitoba Free Press *reported on August 26, 1926, "Bungled in a horrible manner, the hanging of Dan Prociw, murderer of Annie Cardno, his common-law wife, was carried out at dawn yesterday in the yard of the provincial jail. Too long a drop was given by the hangman, and the head of the doomed man was severed from his body."*

Legislative Building

THE LEGISLATIVE BUILDING is so familiar to Manitobans, it is hard to imagine that once there was another building in its place.

The Legislative Building was officially opened in 1920, having weathered nine years of studies, delays and scandals. The process had started in 1911 when it was decided by the government of Premier Rodmond Roblin that the 1882 Legislative Building (see Lost Treasures, page 50) was inadequate to the needs of the growing province, both in terms of size but also in terms of architectural character. The old "Leg" was felt to be too modest a statement for such an important province.

In late 1911 a competition was inaugurated to solicit designs for the new building. Conditions of the competition were prepared by C.H. Dancer, Deputy Minister of the Department of Public Works and the provincial Architect Victor Horwood under the direction of the Honorable Colin Campbell, Minister of Public Works. The assessor selected to adjudicate the competition was Leonard Stokes, a former President of the Royal Institute of British Architects. The committee to confirm the assessor's selection was chosen by Premier Roblin and comprised members of both parties of the House.

Of the 67 designs presented to the competition, five were short-listed for further review (all illustrated here). In theory, any one of these could have been chosen.

A quick perusal of the options shows some of the limits of contemporary thought regarding the appropriate architectural vocabulary for major public buildings. Four of the five entrants picked a large central dome to give their building dignity and grace, and all of them used Classical features and details to convey nobility and grace. However, it is fascinating to observe the impressive variety of dome results within their strict Classical vocabulary.

When the assessor had finished his work, he announced his selection: the design prepared by Frank Simon and Henry Boddington of Liverpool, England.

It is hard to argue with Mr. Stokes' selection of the Simon-Boddington design. The dome is tall, regal, commanding. The working areas of the building are efficiently laid out and the external treatment is calm and dignified.

The competition rendering of Simon and Boddington's winning design for the new Legislative Building.

The scheme submitted by the Toronto firm Sharp and Brown proposed a building with a very strong horizontal emphasis. The long façade was effectively broken into five bays, the central one containing the main entrance and highlighted with a virtual forest of Doric columns.

Clemesha and Portnall, a firm out of Regina, came up with an interesting design, with a distinctive cross-shaped plan and a central dome. That dome, however, appeared squat compared with the Simon-Boddington scheme, and a projecting entrance section exuded modesty rather than grandeur.

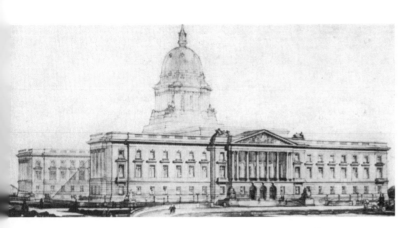

The Maxwell Brothers (Edward and William) of Montreal, famed in Winnipeg for their 1904 design for the Higgins Street station for the Canadian Pacific Railway, produced a design that was remarkably reminiscent of the winner. The H-shaped plan, the powerful central dome, even the articulation of the walls were similar. One significant difference involved the entrance portico, which in the Maxwell design was fussier, with three small doorways situated beneath the grand temple section.

TOO BIG

The design programme developed for the competition called for the Legislative Chamber to accommodate 125 Members of the Legislative Assembly. That number was reflective of the ambitions and expectations that characterized provincial thinking at this time. As Provincial Architect Victor Horwood noted in his article describing the design competition for Construction, "The Province of Manitoba, whose boundaries have been considerably extended, is looking forward to the completion of the Hudson Bay railroad and a direct route to the ocean. What architect could not be inspired with the conditions as set forth in this contest, for while the building is in the process of construction the province itself will extend its frontier a thousand miles, developing its immense resources both in agriculture and mining, and this new territory, which until recently has been nothing but a waste, will soon become a land of promise for the husbandman." In 1912 that optimism was not misplaced; the province's population and economy were still growing at an impressive rate. By the time the building was completed, however, in 1920, the province had suffered incalculable blows. The first came with World War I, whose massive destruction of life knocked the stuffing out of the whole country. Then came the opening of the Panama Canal in 1914, which changed trade routes and undermined Manitoba's economy. To date the Legislative Chamber never held more than 57 members.

TOO MUCH

A major construction project like the Legislative Building involved a great deal of money. For some people, the temptation to exploit the system proved to be an opportunity too good to resist. There had been grumbling early on of cost overruns and sloppy building practices. The prime suspect, and the only person convicted of wrong-doing, was the building's primary contractor, Thomas Kelly. In hearings in 1916 it was proven that he bilked the government for thousands of dollars, mainly through shoddy construction practices and inflated receipts. At one point it was noted that he had charged $230,100 for work that others estimated should have cost $95,000. Kelly served a jail term, but ended his days in Beverly Hills, California, after resuming his building career in the United States.

There were other victims of the scandal. The government of Rodmond Roblin, which had commenced the project, was forced to resign in 1915, and several cabinet ministers were tried, but not convicted. Victor Horwood, the Provincial Architect overseeing construction, was dismissed.

When it was finally opened, in 1920, the Legislative Building had cost more than $9 million; comparable buildings in Alberta and Saskatchewan constructed around the same time cost about $2 million.

With their design Brown and Vallance, of Montreal, chose a highly ornamented clock tower, rather than the popular dome, to symbolize democratic institutions. That powerful vertical was then contrasted with an extremely vibrant façade, distinguished with colonnades, and anchored at the corners with cube shapes that were carefully modeled with niches, windows, cornices and columns.

Brandon Court House

THERE ARE FEW PLACES IN MANITOBA that have the natural site advantages of Brandon. Straddling the broad Assiniboine River Valley, both south and north ends of the city enjoy dramatic views. The potential for making a grand statement with the placement of public buildings on the valley slopes was an opportunity that politicians and architects were loathe to ignore. So it was in the early 1880s, when it was decided that a piece of land on Louise Avenue, east of 1st Street, with an expansive view to the north, was the perfect spot to locate the new court house and an adjoining jail.

At first, the local citizenry was not particularly impressed with the proposal. While it was generally acknowledged that the site was an excellent one, many felt that its situation, on the east side of town, was terribly inconvenient. One newspaper of the day complained, sarcastically, that, "In making this report everything [has been] taken into consideration; the length of the grass in summer and the depth of snow in winter; the variableness of the winds; the view looking toward the river and the view looking away from the river; the proximity to the clouds; the rain fall; the varying degree of temperature – everything, in fact but the convenience of the public in doing business at the offices; that is the last and least consideration."

Despite the controversy, construction on the court house, and adjoining jail, commenced in the summer of 1883. In time, as the building began to take shape, even the formerly antagonistic press admitted that "visitors to the site state that the location was not so far, after all the arguments and hard words which [had] been made." The writer conceded that the "lively appearance of the construction site, the very handsome and massive building with its design and general arrangement reflect great credit upon C. Osborne Wickenden, the architect and Mr. T. Timewell [a Brandon architect], his representative on the work."

C. Osborne Wickenden's design for the Brandon Court House and Jail, built between 1883 and 1884, was a masterful performance, with the serious, elegant building perched impressively at the end of a series of stairs, and surrounded with terraced lawns and carefully tended gardens.

BY THE NECK UNTIL YOU ARE DEAD

Only one woman has been put to death in Manitoba, and it was at the Brandon Jail that she met her fate. The story was a painful one, and roused considerable controversy and sympathy throughout the province. The perpetrator was a young immigrant from England, Emily Blake, who was convicted of killing her employee Mary Lane, wife of a Brandon businessman. Even though she confessed to the crime, there were grave concerns about her mental health, and also of the possibility that the victim's husband might have been involved. Various groups, including the Brandon Women's Christian Temperance Society, lobbied for a commutation of the death sentence. All appeals were declined and on December 27, 1899 the young woman was hanged, apparently without protest.

Brandon Fire Station

THE PRESUMED function of the impressive towers that mark community fire halls is rooted in childhood conjecture. Who didn't think that the tower was the place from which firefighters perched, on the lookout for tell-tale smoke plumes? Or maybe it was the place where they could most effectively call out the alarm?

The tower actually fulfilled a much more mundane function: drying hoses. It makes sense – how else could the sopping wet hoses get dry?

Fire halls still command respect and affection, and whether we know its real purpose or not, it's the tower that often is the repository for those feelings. One of the province's finest fire stations, and one of the most elegant towers, was built in Brandon in 1911. In his design, architect W.A. Elliott gave Brandon a fitting symbol of the firefighter's valour and forthrightness.

Architect W.A. Elliott conceived of Brandon's Central Fire Station in two simple forms, and then employed two distinctly different architectural vocabularies to further distinguish them. The station itself, a big solid block, was a simplified Chateauesque design, notable for its tall hipped roof and elegantly curved dormer window. The tower was carried out in the Italianate Revival style, the perfect choice for such a feature, as that style was known best for its towers, with their heavy flat roofs and powerfully carved brackets. The delicate railings that cover the openings at the top of the tower only enhance the misperception that firefighters used the tower for surveying the city for signs of fire.

LOCAL CONTROVERSY

In an early example of heritage activism, the decision to build Brandon's new fire station roused the anger and opposition of various local citizens, who saw the destruction of the perfectly serviceable old station from 1882 as short-sighted. Architect Walter Shillinglaw was foremost among the protestors, asserting that the proposal was "an act of vandalism of a perfectly needless nature."

HAPPY NEW HOMES

Old fire halls are sometimes converted for alternate uses. Their open plans allow for the introduction of a variety of new uses. Maybe it's the romance of the fire hall itself, linked with heroism, that inspires others. In any event, in Winnipeg, more than ten surplus fire halls have been rehabilitated, several of them for residential uses.

Minto Armoury

DURING MANITOBA'S FORMATIVE YEARS, when there were immediate military requirements and threats—Fenians from the United States briefly invaded the province in the 1880s and Louis Riel was fomenting rebellion to the West—the military commanded respect. Guns, uniforms and flags were familiar and beloved symbols of British power and manly service. Even churches were often festooned with war regalia.

In terms of military architecture, the primary site in Manitoba was the Fort Osborne Barracks in Winnipeg. Originally located in the heart of the city, at the corner of Broadway and Osborne, Fort Osborne was a complex of barracks, stables, storage buildings and a drill hall. All were made of wood, not exactly the kind of material to inspire confidence in one's military.

After World War I, Fort Osborne was abandoned in favour of the former Agricultural College in Tuxedo. With stately brick buildings, it seemed a much more fitting place.

Prior to the War, various other facilities were being built to accommodate the needs of the growing ranks of professional and reserve soldiers. The Minto Armoury, built in 1913 to the designs of architect Herbert Matthews, was the biggest and most architecturally sophisticated of several such buildings. Originally the home to the Royal Winnipeg Rifles, the building's impressive and forbidding outer countenance suited its purpose, although the interior is mostly empty space, a huge drill hall used for training and military tattoos.

A FIGHTING WE WILL GO

Because it has a military purpose—to protect soldiers and house weapons—there is only one way to get into Minto Armoury: through the huge main door. Other smaller doors are not even equipped with knobs on the outside. In order for artillery and vehicles to quickly and easily move in and out, steps were excluded from this part of the design.

Minto Armoury exudes a fortress quality. The walls are thick and strong, of red brick with limestone highlights. The stout corner towers are capped with stylized battlements, remnants of medieval castle architecture. Even the windows, heavily paned and outlined with broad surrounds, look solid and unbreachable. The fact that the doors, so often a welcoming feature in a building, are here not only small but disguised within the general fenestration pattern, makes the building look impregnable.

Dominion Post Office

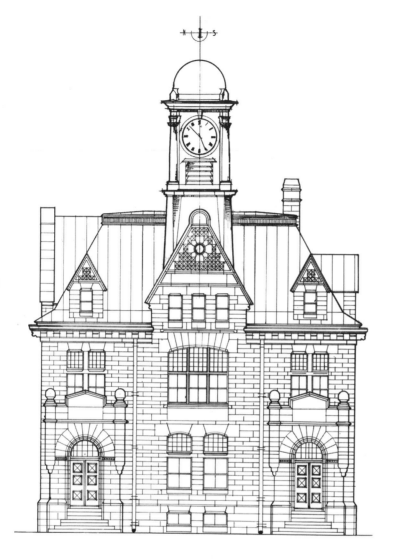

In this architect's drawing the impressive design qualities of the Dominion Post Office in Portage la Prairie are evident. Architect Thomas Fuller, of the federal Department of Public Works, created an exceptional Romanesque Revival-style building, whose rough stone surfaces and muscular details created a handsome and stately presence on Saskatchewan Avenue. The clock tower sketched here was never built.

IT WAS AN INDICATION OF ITS IMPORTANCE to the development of Canada that the post office was one of the first federal government departments formed after Confederation. The service was critical for the development of commerce, and also for maintaining social links in a country whose population was spread over thousands of kilometres.

Postal services were often placed in commercial outlets, and the coveted contract from the government ensured a steady flow of business for the lucky few. For those communities vying for selection as the sites of major post offices, the opportunities for increased traffic, and the location of an expensive new building in town, made competition fierce.

Impressive post offices, sometimes combined with a customs function, went up in several Manitoba communities. In their designs, the architects of the federal government in Ottawa were cognizant of the need to create buildings that were not only functional, but also symbolic of the wealth and sophistication of the new country. Morden, Carman, Souris, Brandon, Stonewall, Selkirk, Virden, Minnedosa and Dauphin boasted grand post offices, which contrasted with a background of a pioneer architectural landscape. The Dominion Post Office that rose in Portage la Prairie between 1895-98 was the finest post office of all.

The post office in Portage la Prairie had the distinction of being designed by one of Canada's most famous architects at the time, Thomas Fuller. He was responsible for the design of the country's first Parliament Building, built from 1859 to 1866 and destroyed by fire in 1916. The one surviving section of that complex, the Library of Parliament, is still one of the most beautiful buildings in Canada.

In 1960 Portage la Prairie's city council decided to convert the old post office for use as the new city hall.

MANITOBA'S FIRST POST OFFICE

In Manitoba, the first postal service was established in 1855 in the home of William Ross and is now preserved in Winnipeg as a museum by the Manitoba Historical Society. A secure monthly mail service could only be accomplished between the Red River Settlement and Pembina, North Dakota. Not until 1885, with the arrival of the Canadian Pacific Railway, was an all-Canadian mail route established.

Lost Treasures — Official Buildings

GOVERNMENTS COME AND GOVERNMENTS GO. That's democracy. But the institutions remain – political parties, laws, bureaucracy. While we may look upon the present collection of buildings that house the institutions of government (Legislative Building, court houses, jails) it is no surprise to learn that buildings, like governments, have also come and gone. The examples here represent exceptional monuments, now gone, that once were integral parts of our architectural landscape.

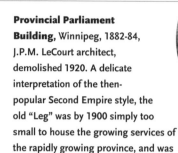

Provincial Parliament Building, Winnipeg, 1882-84, J.P.M. LeCourt architect, demolished 1920. A delicate interpretation of the then-popular Second Empire style, the old "Leg" was by 1900 simply too small to house the growing services of the rapidly growing province, and was replaced by our current Legislative Building.

In this more enlightened age, the designation of "lunatic" has left the public vocabulary. When it was built, in 1883-86, however, the **Lunatic Asylum** in Selkirk was state-of-the-art, both in its architecture, by C. Osborne Wickenden, and its psychiatric treatments. It was demolished in 1978.

Winnipeg City Hall, 1886, Barber and Barber architects, demolished 1964. This fabulous Victorian edifice was a beloved city landmark that fell to desires of politicians and designers who sought to invigorate the area with massive monuments to the modern.

Post Office, Winnipeg, 1904-09, Darling and Pearson,
demolished after the Post Office relocated to St. Mary's Avenue.

Emerson Town Hall, 1881,
demolished 1917. At the time of
the construction of its town hall,
Emerson considered itself a rival
to Winnipeg. The routing of the
Canadian Pacific Railway into
Winnipeg dashed those hopes,
but for almost 40 years the grand
building was a reminder of what
could have been.

Court House, Winnipeg, original section (right), 1882-83, C.O. Wickenden architect,
burned 1957; addition (left) 1893-94, C.H. Wheeler, demolished 1965. The original
building, a highly sophisticated Second Empire-style design, was enlarged within ten
years by a building with a completely different, and by then more popular, architecture:
Victorian Gothic.

Postal, Customs and Inland Revenue Building, Brandon, 1889-90,
demolished 1970s. A beautiful building, the old four-storey post office
was a fine example of Romanesque Revival architecture.

Chapter 4

CHURCHES

St. Andrew's-on-the-Red Anglican Church

IT'S THE SPRING OF 1845. It's cold. It's wet. Two men, both European, stand near a majestic, wide, sweeping arc of fast-flowing water. With the Red River behind them, they pace, muttering and gesturing to each other, as they face a wide prairie field. William Cockran, Archdeacon, is a Church of England clergyman arrived from England to serve the religious needs of the settlement at Red River. His task: to continue the work of establishing the Anglican Church in the colony. The other man, Duncan McRae, is an irascible Scottish stonemason who is familiar with the terrain. McRae has been involved with the construction of dozens of major buildings in the area, most notably the erection of the walls of Lower Fort Garry.

Today, the men are here to decide where the new church will sit, which way it will face, its size and its dimensions.

Archdeacon Cockran, a man of the cloth and of forceful will, is determined to create a large building, with a nave long enough to accommodate hundreds of the faithful. McRae, knowledgeable in the ways of stone and mortar is, to say the least, skeptical that a church so grand will come to be.

According to legend, McRae argues that the church Cockran envisions is far too long for the human voice, specifically that of the Archdeacon's, to carry. But Cockran disagrees. He insists the mason stand where the back of the church is projected to be. He blazes forth his first sermon on that very spot. "Duncan McRae," he bellows, "they tell me that you drink more rum than is good for you. In future, curb your bestial desires and try to live a sober, righteous and Godly life." McRae, stung, but still in control of his wit, replies that in fact, contrary to his former opinion, "the church is nae long enough." And so, the long nave came to be.

The legend dramatizes the age old balance between practical considerations and lofty ideals, and negotiations between client and architect. In 1845 ideas became buildings without today's preparatory drawings, without floor plans, without renderings of important details. Archdeacon Cockran merely specified the building size, perhaps by counting his steps or leaving four rocks on the ground to mark the corners. He might have indicated the general architectural character he desired (in this case, Gothic Revival, reminiscent of churches in his homeland) and he probably placed extra attention on the design of the spire. But, in the end, it was Duncan McRae and his crew who would have made both practical and aesthetic decisions, from the wall thickness to the size of the window openings and the detail stone work around the front doors. And, of course, that disputed nave.

In 1999 St. Andrew's Anglican Church celebrated its 150th anniversary, making it the oldest church in Western Canada. While it is not known whether he celebrated its completion with a sip of rum, the church has withstood the test of time, a testament to the fine craftsmanship of its builder, Duncan McRae.

DUNCAN MCRAE

Duncan McRae, the master stonemason who oversaw construction of St. Andrew's, paid dearly for his work there. First, it might have bruised his religious sensibility, to be working on an Anglican church when he was a staunch Presbyterian. He and his other co-religionists would have to wait a quarter of a century for the construction in 1870 of Little Britain Presbyterian Church, just south of Lower Fort Garry, for their needs to be met. Secondly, and more tragically, he suffered serious injuries while working on St. Andrew's Church. He fell almost 21 metres from scaffolding and while he recovered, he never again was able to do any of the heavy labour at his other projects.

The word *Dynevor* was initially attached to the parish rectory, built in 1865. Archdeacon Abraham Cowley added the word during his tenure there. It was a formal title given to a childhood friend and mentor. The name eventually was also applied to the nearby post office and finally to the church itself.

St. Peter's Dynevor Anglican Church

THE ROUGH STONE WALLS, the elegant spire and of course the pointed Gothic windows of St. Peter's Dynevor Anglican Church all suggest British roots, and a British congregation. But the suggestion is misleading, at least in terms of the people the building served. It is actually connected to Aboriginal peoples who, under the leadership of Chief Peguis, built it and worshipped there for more than 50 years.

Chief Peguis led bands of Saulteaux (also called Ojibway) and Cree who camped near the banks of Netley Creek, a tributary of the Red River, and an area which offered abundant sources of fish and game. The arrival in 1812 of Lord Selkirk's Scottish crofters at the forks of the Red and Assiniboine rivers lead to the establishment of a fledgling farming economy, and a way of life that was to be a harbinger for the influx of European culture that would change Peguis' people's lives forever.

By the early 1830s Selkirk's settlers were more comfortably established near the Forks. Archdeacon William Cockran of England, who was working to establish a church at the St. Andrew's Rapids, turned his attentions to the Aboriginals at Netley Creek. First he focused on encouraging them to begin farming and in the spring of 1832 Chief Peguis and several other Aboriginal families agreed to participate in Cockran's farming experiment. By 1849 the Aboriginal population of the settlement had grown to 460, with 93 hectares of land under cultivation.

Cockran's second objective—for religious activity and subsequent conversion—had been inaugurated back in 1836 with the construction of a log church. Conversions, however, were slow in coming, even though Peguis was baptized as an Anglican on February 7, 1838, choosing as his Christian name William King (his descendants adopted the surname "Prince"). In 1851, having returned to the settlement after a convalescent absence, Cockran worked with Peguis to erect a more durable stone church. Cockran designed the building and supervised the construction. Stones were quarried from the Garson area and they were shaped at St. Peter's by Aboriginal craftsmen under the watchful eye of master stonemason Duncan McRae. The resulting building, completed in 1854, is a unique collaboration that fused the European and Aboriginal aspirations of the day.

CHIEF PEGUIS

Chief Peguis (1774-1864) was a revered Aboriginal leader who became a trusted friend and benefactor to the Selkirk Settlers. Although he is buried at St. Peter's, his actual resting place is unmarked. Instead a fine, red granite stone commemorates his life.

Holy Trinity Anglican Church

IN 1883 WHEN ARCHITECT CHARLES WHEELER PRESENTED his winning design to the building committee of Winnipeg's Holy Trinity Anglican Church, there was the expectation that this magnificent building would rise in all its Gothic glory.

The Parish of Holy Trinity had been formed in 1868 and successive modest wooden buildings near Portage Avenue and Fort Street had served parishioners over the years. In 1883, however, the decision was made to move to a new site at the corner of Donald Street and Graham Avenue. The church undertook an international design competition for their new building, with a prize of $300 for the winner, Charles H. Wheeler, an architect newly arrived in Winnipeg from England.

Construction commenced on the church in 1883 and it was officially opened August 4, 1884 by the Archbishop of Rupert's Land, His Excellency Robert Machray. An article of the day noted that the church walls were built with "Stony Mountain limestone, from a picked strata of bluish-grey tint, the dressings and buttresses of Selkirk limestone, and all the apexes, bases, crosses, labels, etc., are worked in Ohio stone, which the severity of our winters has sobered down, and [which] is now in harmony with the colors of the native limestone." It is a building of rare quality, whose every detail was clearly considered.

If you're familiar with downtown Winnipeg, especially the corner of Donald and Graham, you probably don't recognize the architect's presentation drawing shown at the right. That's because the dominating feature of the church, the towering spire, was not built. The congregation had started their project with the highest of hopes, in 1883, at a time when the province's economy was strong. By the late 1880s Manitoba was struggling through a recession that lasted for several years and brought many a dream to heel. The $163,200 paid for the church likely would have doubled with the addition of the tower. That was a cost the church simply could not bear. Even in 1897, however, in an article published in the *Canadian Architect and Builder*, architect George Gouinlock assumed the tower still would go up, and noted that a "temporary bell structure somewhat disfigures the view from his point." It's a harsh assessment, but one that holds some truth.

Even without its spire, Holy Trinity Anglican Church is one of the highlights of Gothic church architecture in Manitoba. This photograph of the southeast corner, taken around 1884, shows the talent of architect Charles Wheeler at his prime.

MISSING SPIRE

The architect's presentation drawing of 1883 is instructive about the kind of artistic license Wheeler employed to impress his clients. Human figures placed outside the fence give the impression that the church was about 100 metres tall. A more accurate rendering would have seen these figures almost double in size. But then you'd have to admit that the church would not have looked nearly as powerful.

St. Mary's Roman Catholic Cathedral

FOR 15 YEARS THE CONGREGATION OF ST. MARY'S Roman Catholic Cathedral in Winnipeg was apparently satisfied with their church. A solid, respectable building of brick, it was a model of Romanesque Revival styling. The front façade was particularly redolent of the precepts of the style. Architect C. Balston Kenway seems to have looked long and hard at the simplest of 11th-century Romanesque churches, recreating in 1880 a tough, clean surface whose heaviness and starkness recalled the weight of early Christianity struggles.

By the mid-1890s, something had happened. Kenway's simple façade was no longer satisfying, but rather was seen by many in the congregation as dated and ineffective. In 1896 the church called on Samuel Hooper, then gaining a name for himself as a talented and resourceful designer, to create a completely new façade. The result was a startling departure from Kenway's original conception.

Hooper respected the basic Romanesque character of the building, but just barely. Round arches and heavy brick work, two hallmarks of Romanesque Revival, were employed, but otherwise Hooper responded with a more Victorian response to that style. That meant resorting to a much greater variety: of forms (like the two dramatically shaped towers that flank the entrance section), materials, roof shapes (like the tall spire on the bell tower and the conical roof on the west wing), window and door openings, and especially details, too numerous to name.

What was accomplished at St. Mary's was a striking contrast to the situation around the corner at Holy Trinity Anglican Church (opposite), built around the same time. Where the congregation at Holy Trinity was unable to build the tower that would have made that church a wonder to behold, those at St. Mary's were fortunate enough to be able to undertake a whole new building project, and within fifteen years to create the look of a brand new church.

FACE LIFT!

It's hard to believe, but these two images are of the same building. At right, C. Balston Kenway's modest 1880 design for St. Mary's. Above, sixteen years later, Samuel Hooper's energetic obliteration of Kenway's face.

St. Francois Xavier Roman Catholic Church

PERHAPS CUTHBERT GRANT, THE MAN WHO in 1824 founded Grantown, the predecessor to St. Francois Xavier, would have been impressed with this church's stately elegance. It's also possible that the man acknowledged to be the first leader of the Métis people might have seen in the elegant brick façade a betrayal of his cause. It might have been to him a symbol of just the kind of eastern Canadian presence in Manitoba he had devoted much of his life to fighting.

For more than 40 years, Cuthbert Grant struggled to secure a place for the Métis in a rapidly changing world. At each dramatic step in the evolution of the province in the first half of the 19th century, Cuthbert Grant was there, fighting to secure and preserve a home for them. It was Grant who worked to carve out a place for his people. First, as the Métis ally and benefactor, the Northwest Company, was swallowed up by the Hudson's Bay Company, then as the hated Red River Settlement grew to stability, and finally as eastern Canadian influences inched into the territory. Finally with a pleasant, fertile stretch of land along the Assiniboine River—about 20 kilometres west of the Red River Settlement—secured for a Métis settlement he must have thought his prayers were answered. Grantown thrived and in 1833 he had a substantial log church built.

By the time Grant died in 1854 other leaders, like Louis Riel Sr. had taken up the Métis cause and were critical of the HBC monopoly, and of Grant's relationship with that symbol of English power and the fur trade economy. Grant likely died an unhappy man, although his burial place under the altar of the church recalled the reverence still accorded the great man.

Forty-six years after his death, when this church rose over the old log one, the world of Cuthbert Grant was no more. Manitoba was full of immigrants from eastern Canada and Europe. The Métis cause had been thwarted and then destroyed. Even the community of Grantown had ceased to exist. It was renamed St. Francois Xavier, and many of the former inhabitants had been bought out, moving further west in search of a homeland.

The Roman Catholic Church at St. Francois Xavier was built in 1900 to the designs of Joseph Senecal, the architect of choice for Roman Catholic churches in Manitoba. It's an exquisite example of the type of church then rising in many Franco-Manitobain communities. A soaring spire of delicate design can be seen for several kilometres, while up close the attention to the details of the brick work suggest just how important this building was for the community.

CUTHBERT GRANT (1793-1854)

Before the great Métis leader Louis Riel there was Cuthbert Grant. Born to a Métis mother and a partner in the North West Company (the primary rival in the fur trade to the Hudson's Bay Company (HBC)), Cuthbert Grant was a powerful figure in the early history of Manitoba. Often portrayed as someone who was used by both the NWC and the HBC in their efforts to protect their business interests, Grant was just as likely a shrewd observer, and pragmatic actor, given the circumstances of the day. Where Louis Riel (see page 15) chose to work outside the system, and fomented rebellion, seizing government in 1870, Cuthbert Grant preferred to work within the system, affecting changes that for years accorded the Métis a comfortable place at Red River. Originally linked to the NWC, he was appointed "Captain General" of the Métis and was a key player in the fierce competition between the NWC and the HBC in the early 1800s. That was a competition that in 1816 turned deadly, with Grant leading a group of Métis against a group of Selkirk Settlers at the Battle of Seven Oaks, which left 21 of the settlers dead. Grant was never punished, which points to his considerable influence.

The cultural origins of the builders of Grund can be read into the design of the church's tower and in the composition of its interior.

It was in the tower and steeple that carpenters Hallgrimson and Sveinsson recalled their northern European and Scandinavian roots. The steeple design below, an elegant candle snuff shape, was a popular choice in northern European countries like Germany, Sweden and Norway. Scandinavian (or Viking) influences were expressed in the decorative criss-cross shapes at the top edge of the tower, surely an homage to the twined shapes found on so many Scandinavian objects.

Inside, the simple character of the church nave, protected by the gentle arch of the ceiling, is a loving testament to the tenets of Lutheranism.

Grund Lutheran Church

THE OLDEST ICELANDIC LUTHERAN CHURCH IN MANITOBA is not located where one might suspect: at Gimli, Hecla, Arborg, or Riverton. In other words, it is not located in the main centres of New Iceland, the colony established in 1875 on the shores of Lake Winnipeg that saw the arrival of hundreds of Icelanders to Manitoba. In fact, the province's oldest standing Icelandic church, built in 1889, stands at Grund, a south-central area of Manitoba better known for its French and Belgian settlements.

The story of this church begins in August of 1880 when Sigurdur Christopherson and Kristjan Jonsson set out for the Tiger Hills district, currently the Rural Municipality of Argyle. The two men were impressed by reports from a mutual friend Everett Parsonage, about the area's fertile and arable land. Perfect land, it would seem, for agricultural pursuits. In March of 1881 the first party of Icelandic settlers undertook the journey to this new "Paradise." The trip, which commenced in Gimli, was 323 kilometres in length, took 16 days to complete, and was undertaken mostly on foot across snow and ice. By 1883 the settlement consisted of 17 Icelandic families. Sigurdur Christopherson continued in his immigration efforts, persuading prospective settlers in New Iceland, Ontario and even Iceland, to venture to Argyle. By 1890, 700 Icelanders lived in the district.

Religious services and scriptural readings at the new settlement were held each evening in every Icelandic home, as was the custom in the homeland. By 1884, however, with a solid population base intact, it was apparent that a formal church was needed, and on January 1st, 1884 the Frelsis Lutheran Church was formed.

Construction on the church building concluded in 1889. Two skilled carpenters—Byring Hallgrimson and Arnie Sveinsson—oversaw the work. While it is a typical pioneer church building in many ways, incorporating a basic Gothic vocabulary typical for Protestant churches, with pointed windows and doors, a rose window and tracery, as seen here in the second stage of the tower, the church at Grund is also distinctly Lutheran, and distinctly Icelandic.

WHAT'S A GRUND?

The Icelandic language symbolizes the nation, its history and literature. Many settlers who struggled through daunting winter conditions on the shores of Lake Winnipeg often took time to compose poetry and prose in their native tongue. The Icelandic words included here, Grund and Frelsis mean, respectively, "grassy plain" and "freedom."

St. Paul's Anglican Church

TOPOGRAPHICAL FEATURES of Churchill, Manitoba, and its surrounding area are not easily transformed into building materials. Located far above the treeline, surface maps show a region etched by a severe climate; flat, barren and snow-laden for most of the year. Natural building materials include stone (as was the material of choice for Prince of Wales's Fort, page 42); ice, when it's cold enough, or animal skins used by Aboriginals and Inuit.

Europeans in the area relied on shipments of building materials from "away" for their projects. And so it was that the people undertaking the construction of St. Paul's Anglican Church found their materials from "away," although in this case "away" meant England and the material wasn't traditional wood. In its place was pre-fabricated iron. While three other pre-fabricated iron structures made their way to Canada's north, St. Paul's Anglican Church at Churchill is the only one that remains.

The church traces its roots to the Church Missionary Society, or C.M.S., an Anglican organization formed in 1799 charged with providing religious instruction to those at the far corners of the earth. In Canada this meant the conversion of Aboriginals. In 1882 the C.M.S. dispatched Reverend J.J. Lofthouse from England to create a mission at Churchill on the saltwater shores of the icy Hudson Bay. He commenced his task in 1886, having been waylaid at the more southerly-located, and now mostly inaccessible, York Factory for several years.

As part of its missionary work, the C.M.S. created a building program that provided outposts with acceptable church buildings. One scheme saw the creation of the pre-fabricated metal building that Reverend Lofthouse ordered in 1889. The crates bearing the metal structural pieces arrived in 1890, but it would take him and his congregation three more years to assemble the building.

When it was finally finished, the church served as both residence for Reverend Lofthouse and the place of worship for his congregation, composed of local Aboriginals and Hudson's Bay Company workers. The building was so small that each Sunday Reverend Lofthouse packed-up and moved his personal belongings to make room for wooden bench pews brought in to seat the faithful.

In this photograph taken around 1900 the church looks at first glance like a wooden building, with boards attached and aligned vertically. But they belie the true story. Seams running horizontally along the side of the church indicate the places where the metal panels meet and the perfectly smooth roof was in fact a series of large metal sheets

MORE HEAVY METAL

Few early builders experimented with metal in Manitoba. The best known building incorporating metal structure and design was the Empire Hotel (built in 1881-83), whose cast iron façade was dismantled in 1981 and placed in storage. A portion of the façade was instituted as a decorative panel at the Centre Cultural Franco-Manitobain in St. Boniface.

Emerson Baptist Church

STONE, WHETHER IT BE GRANITE, sandstone or limestone, is a durable and visually impressive building material. It is difficult to work with and expensive, but it endures. But what if you desire the "look" of stone, but possess neither the time, money or skill to build from stone?

At the turn of the century, in Manitoba you'd have been in luck, because for about a decade crews of itinerant craftsmen roamed the country with special moulds and other equipment with which they would produce a building that looked like it was created from stone, but was actually formed from concrete.

Residents of the town of Emerson, located near the Canada - United States border south of Winnipeg, were enamoured of the stuff. Between about 1895 and 1910 at least a dozen concrete block buildings were erected in Emerson. Homebuilders were the most common implementers of the blocks although even the members of the congregation of the local Baptist Church found themselves in its thrall.

In 1905-06, based on an architectural design by well known Winnipeg architect Hugh McCown, a handsome stone-like church building rose, a sturdy addition to Emerson's stock of local churches, of which all were made from wood or brick.

t's only when you get up close, and observe the quality of the "stonework," its perfectly straight courses and crisp edges, that he real material—concrete blocks—becomes apparent.

MOULD-A-STONE

This contraption, a typical block-making device, was at the very heart of the building process. Soft, wet concrete was poured into the container's cavity. The container was easily fitted with one of several exterior facing plates. Plates were designed to represent such things as stones, plant forms, or scrollwork. For the builders of concrete block structures the variety of mould facades presented all sorts of possibilities to customers. They could choose a single façade treatment or a configuration or combination of facades, each of which would provide a wholly unique look. At the Emerson Baptist Church the building committee selected the popular rock-face finish.

Westminster United Church

AROUND THE TURN OF THE CENTURY, when Presbyterians in Manitoba began replacing the first generation of their churches with larger, new monuments of stone, they invariably looked to one man to interpret their architectural aspirations: J.H.G. Russell.

Russell designed three landmark Presbyterian churches in Winnipeg between 1903 and 1914, and they are three of Winnipeg's finest architectural treasures. Augustine was constructed first in 1903-04, followed by Westminster in 1911-12, and finally, Knox was constructed from 1914-17. Together they form an unparalleled combination of faith, optimism and wealth.

With each structure, Russell captured different elements of what was called the Gothic Revival style. Gothic Revival was developed in the 18th century as a movement aimed at reviving the spirit and forms of the Middle Ages (about 1200 a.d. to 1500 a.d.), especially those of France and England. The movement was profound and pervasive, affecting literature (Sir Walter Scott's *Ivanhoe*), visual arts (the Pre-Raphaelites), decorative arts and crafts, and architecture. For Victorian-era architects, Medieval Gothic was seen as exemplary, not only in terms of its engineering feats, especially the creation of unbelievably large and high churches, but also as a source of morality, spirituality and craftsmanship.

In Canada, the Gothic Revival was embraced as a connection to Great Britain and also as a design style that was suitable for a harsher climate. The Parliament Buildings in Ottawa are pre-eminent examples of Gothic Revival architecture. By the time Gothic Revival architecture reached Manitoba in the late 19th century, the form had lost some of its former expressive power, but was still considered the requisite architectural expression for many churches. Major Protestant faiths, particularly, employed the style to highlight their affinity with Great Britain. Even the smallest of rural Protestant churches featured pointed windows to identify that heritage. For a large, complex church like Westminster Presbyterian, however, it was necessary to look to someone who was a knowledgeable and sensitive interpreter of Gothic's rich and varied possibilities. The man for the job was J.H.G. Russell.

At Westminster, Russell appears to have looked to the church's London namesake Westminster Abbey and its Medieval Gothic character for guidance. Accordingly his design reflects a similarly elongated floor plan and pinnacled towers as the main organizing elements. He then rendered the entire building by coalescing an array of traditional Gothic forms and details into a strong and soaring expression of power and spirit.

In this exquisite presentation drawing you can find a little historical footnote, in a title bar across the bottom. The church's location is given as the corner of Maryland and Buell; this latter thoroughfare was renamed, for the church, as Westminster Avenue.

JHG RUSSELL (1862-1946)

Presbyterians weren't the only ones who consistently looked to J.H.G. Russell for his architectural talents. From his arrival in Winnipeg in 1894, and for 50 years after, he was one of Winnipeg's most celebrated architects. Russell was for many of the city's movers and shakers the architect-of-choice. J.H. Ashdown, the hardware magnate, called on Russell for almost every building he needed, from his warehouse and store, to his various houses and mansions. Russell also designed important Winnipeg landmarks like the Y.M.C.A. and Child's Building (see page 93). He was President, in 1912-13, of the Royal Architectural Institute of Canada.

St Elie Romanian Orthodox Church

FOR THOSE UNFAMILIAR with the great variety of traditional church designs around the world, St. Elie Romanian Orthodox Church at Lennard (about 20 kilometres north of Russell) might be mistaken as an early pioneer house. Its banners, however, and various crosses and decoratively pointed windows, not to mention the robed priest standing in the doorway, illuminate its true function as a church. Still, its form is exotic to those eyes accustomed to the basic concept of "church:" formal entrance, spires, highly decorated surfaces.

This church is, in fact, connected to historic architectural traditions, and is Manitoba's oldest Romanian church. Built in 1908 by Romanian pioneers from Bukovyna, then a province of the Austro-Hungarian Empire, this church replaced a sod and log structure dating from 1903. The form of St. Elie—a simple rectangular shape with rounded ends—is derived from centuries-old church designs common in Bukovyna and Romania. Ukrainian pioneers also built several churches in this style. Three still stand. One is at Poplar Point (north of Winnipeg), another near Dauphin, and the other is located near Sirko in south-eastern Manitoba.

The interior of St. Elias Romanian Orthodox Church is, in a word, breathtaking. It's small, yet every centimetre of wall inside the church is covered with various opulent decorations. Richly layered colours characterize the fabric and details of each ornamentation. Pressed tin panels which cover the walls are painted robin's egg blue and provide a background for scores of icon paintings and banners, wood carvings, and crosses. These embellishments make the church one of the most memorable in Manitoba.

Ukrainian Catholic Church of the Immaculate Conception

ON TUESDAY, OCTOBER 29, 1929 the New York Stock Market collapsed. According to tradition, that single event plunged the world into the Great Depression, a decade further marked by climactic calamities, the collapse of the farm economy and subsequently, widespread and abject poverty.

With the economy busted, crops withering in the fields, and dust as a result of droughts lining farmers' cupboards, the stalwart and dedicated group of Ukrainian Catholics at Cooks Creek found both inspiration and time to replace their modest 1904 church with what would become one of the biggest building projects in rural Manitoba.

The impetus sprang forth from the parish priest, Father Philip Ruh. As he noted in a newspaper interview in 1959, "The idea— it came to me one afternoon when I was smoking my pipe in the living room. Everything came to me in a flash of lightning. All at once I had the dimensions worked out in my head—110 feet to the tip of the dome, 150 feet across the chancel—but then alas we had no money."

Father Ruh's eminently practical description of the building— merely as an object of dimensions—surely conceals aesthetic considerations that must have intrigued him as he worked out the design. Care was taken in rendering traditional Ukrainian forms, especially regarding the domes. Then Father Ruh married them with his own unique vision of ecclesiastical architecture. A classical portico at the front doors and Romanesque details like blind arcades encircle the building at the roof line. These manifestations could only be the result of long and careful contemplation.

The Father's reference to the church's poverty was not coy. It was a simple, brutal truth. Still, work on the church boldly began as scheduled. Hundreds of people volunteered their labour. Youths were trained to handle saws and levels; men dug the foundation ditches; women hauled rocks; children carried smaller stones. By 1934 the walls were erected and in 1939 the roof was complete. That same year amateur artists had begun painting the plaster walls. Good progress, but the church would still take another 13 years, until 1952, to finally be completed.

The church features rich, dazzling yellows and blues. On closer approach, dramatically-posed, life-sized statues of biblical characters grace surrounding grounds, an impressive bell tower looms and a small park-like area is enshrined by an ornamental grotto, or caves. From a distance the church is a canvas of rich, deep, textures. Marble abounds.

The huge black domes of the Church of the Immaculate Conception fulfill two functions. They identify the church as Ukrainian Catholic. In Ukrainian, the domes are called *banyas*, and can take a variety of forms. The banyas at Cooks Creek are hemispherical, while many other Ukrainian Catholic churches feature onion-shaped domes, like the one below. The banyas also fulfill a liturgical role as they are metaphors for forms of the public service prescribed by the Church. Consequently, there are nine banyas, representing the nine ranks of the angelic world.

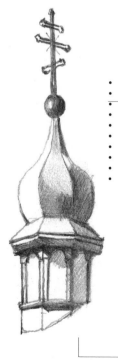

THE NUMBERS GAME

1,000 — the number of people the church can seat

400,000 — the cost, in CDN dollars, estimated by Father Ruh in 1930 for a professional contractor to build the church

5,100,000 — the cost in CDN dollars to build the church in 1999

45,000 — the actual cost in CDN dollars of the church employing the use of volunteers

10 — the size, in acres, of the whole complex (church, grotto, cemetery)

80 — the weight, in tons, of iron for reinforcing

10 — the number of carloads of tiles

1 — the number of carloads of slate

7,000 — the weight, in pounds, of copper for the domes

THE VISIONARY

Father Philip Ruh, O.M.I., was born on a farm in Alsace (France) in 1883 and ordained a priest in 1910. Shortly after his ordination he was assigned to a mission near L'viv, Ukraine (at that time part of Austro-Hungary). While there, he learned to speak Ukrainian and used the opportunity to pursue his interest in architecture, studying the magnificent Baroque churches in the area. If Father Ruh thought his adventures in Ukraine were exciting, he was in for a shock. In 1913 he was sent to northern Alberta to begin to minister to Canadian Ukrainian Catholics.

Peripatetic like most clergy of his day, Father Ruh was repeatedly uprooted throughout his career in western Canada. Most departures, however, were marked by an enduring artifact which expressed Father Ruh's long-held affection for architecture—a church building. His prolific and interesting works made him a much sought after designer of Ukrainian Catholic churches. He was responsible for dozens of churches in Alberta, Saskatchewan, Manitoba and Ontario. By the 1930s his architectural work had become ambitious. Besides his final crowning glory of Cooks Creek, other notable Manitoba Ruh churches can be found in Dauphin, Winnipegosis and Winnipeg.

Upon closer approach the facades of the church begin to change. It is still big and beautiful, capable of catching the eye at every moment. However, suddenly what was marble, or ancient weathered stone is obviously not so. In fact, the finishes are painted onto stucco and concrete. A skillful example of faux finishes, rendered persuasively to recreate the textures and patterns of other finer materials.

Hence, the realities imposed by the Great Depression of the 1930s are in evidence everywhere. The adage "necessity is the mother of invention" was embraced by Father Ruh and his colleagues who during one of history's greatest setbacks, and with no money, created a grand and detailed church by mixing equal parts of devotion, invention, and the paint colours required to create finishes that looked just like marble.

THE GROTTO

Father Ruh coaxed concrete to resemble other materials for the grotto which adjoins the church. Here, the inspiration was the famous grotto site at Lourdes, France, and concrete was shaped (often by hand) to resemble the rough natural stones at Lourdes. The Cooks Creek grotto is a fairly faithful copy of the Lourdes grotto, containing a Calvary (the representation of Christ's crucifixion), and the Stations of the Cross, a series of 14 crosses and accompanying images which commemorate the stages of Christ's journey to Calvary.

Lost Treasures – Churches

AROUND THE WORLD churches and temples comprise some of the finest examples of architecture. They are potent community symbols of man's faith, built both for the gods and as a central meeting place for people. Their designs, modest or grand, often reflect the unique philosophies of those who gather there and their own divine inspiration. The loss of such buildings is a sad thing, in part, because church interiors and exteriors are shared by so many. Whether they are lost due to fire or the evolving population and urban changes that have undermined their viability, the result is always the same. An expression of faith, rich with history and detail, is gone forever.

Saint Boniface Roman Catholic Cathedral. All that is left of this 1908 version of the cathedral in Saint Boniface are its walls. Its Romanesque Revival towers, roof and interior (inset) were consumed by fire in 1968. One of the most memorable conflagrations in recent Winnipeg history raged as thousands of heart-broken citizens witnessed part of their French Catholic heritage destroyed. Only its august limestone walls were salvaged. Marked by extraordinary elegance, the remaining facade still stands facing westward across the Red River. It is most animated and breathtaking when illuminated on a warm prairie evening by the orange and red rays of a brilliant sunset.

Ironically, the sight conjures up images of the very flames that destroyed it. In an inspired decision, sensitive to the symbolic importance of this beloved church, the archdiocese of St. Boniface decided to buttress the scorched walls and to build a smaller church within. This new building — by famed local architect Etienne Gaboury — is a respectful, serene presence, located at the back of the nave and located within the ruins of the original church.

Roman Catholic Church, St. Pierre-Jolys. This exquisite yellow brick church, located in St.-Pierre Jolys located 40 kilometres south of Winnipeg, features walls rendered in Romanesque Revival with Gothic towers. It became the object of bitter debate in the late 1970s with some driving for its replacement and others lobbying for its preservation. The "moderns" won and in 1981 the old church, built in 1899-1904, came down. Devastated parishioners salvaged what they could and parts of the old church now decorate living rooms and basements in homes in St. Pierre-Jolys.

Ukrainian Catholic Church, Mountain Road. The loss by fire in 1966 of this 1923 Ukrainian Baroque church at Mountain Road, 40 kilometres northwest of Neepawa, was a real blow to Manitoba's heritage. Not only was its design impressive, it was constructed of logs, an amazing feat given its enormous size. The designer, Father Philip Ruh, did not shy away from challenging architectural projects, and left behind a legacy of churches, most notably, the one at Cooks Creek (page 64).

Central United Church, Brandon. This red brick, Gothic Brandon landmark, built in 1901 as St. Paul's Presbyterian Church was razed in 1986, in the dead of a brutally cold winter. It had stood for years, one of the proudest achievements of Walter Shillinglaw, Brandon's foremost early architect.

Grace Methodist Church, Winnipeg. It stood, like a beacon, for nearly 75 years, on a little triangle of land where Donald Street, Ellice and Notre Dame avenues intersect, just down the street from the former Knox Presbyterian Church. Built in 1893 and demolished in 1957, the eclectically designed Grace Methodist Church (later United), was created by Manitoba architect James Chisholm. Its dramatic presence, juxtaposed near the grand Knox Presbyterian Church must have created an unparalleled concentration of beauty and power. But Grace Methodist Church could not withstand the threats posed by dwindling numbers in the congregation and a poor location in a swirl of ever-growing traffic. The church was demolished and replaced by a parking lot.

Knox Presbyterian Church, Winnipeg. Demolished in 1914, Knox Presbyterian Church was a superb example of High Victorian Gothic style. Unfortunately it succumbed to Winnipeg's rapidly changing urban complexion in the early 1900s. Simply put, the church was in the wrong place at the wrong time. Built in 1884 based on the designs of the architectural firm Barber and Barber, the church stood at the corner of Donald Street and Ellice Avenue in downtown Winnipeg (near the Walker Theatre). By 1910 its congregation concluded that it was too small and that the neighbourhood was too congested. They decided to construct a new limestone Late Gothic style edifice and selected a site on Edmonton Street across the street from Central Park. The latter church stands there still. The former church was unceremoniously torn down.

Chapter 5

SCHOOLS

Garnett School

FEW SCHOOLS ARE ANYTHING LIKE THIS ONE. It's awkward and weird-looking. And the fact that at least three others like it were built in the Carman area makes it even more intriguing. Garnett School, built around 1890, is very clearly an adaptation of a false-fronted store, altered with a formal entrance appendage. It's a novel solution, given the popularity of more conventional designs: the typical box with a gable roof, for example. That the Garnett design was not only accepted, but then used by at least three more school districts, suggests that someone with a forceful character was shaping the area's school architecture, and thus creating the first "standardized" designs in the province.

Later buildings were slightly more ambitious. The addition of bell towers, brackets, window banks and decorative mouldings, however, only elaborated on the bones of a truly eccentric design concept.

Unfortunately it's impossible to unravel the aesthetic sensibility lurking behind these schools. Old newspapers and school reports yield only the name of a local builder who may have been involved, William Webster of Roland, but nothing about the thinking or information that would shed further light on precedents or intent. Only the images survived as an important legacy.

Whatever their shortcomings, these buildings are Manitoba originals, important footnotes in its history. One must admire the designer, a serious person who built on their experience, changing the design with each new project, adapting, tweaking, improving.

Garnett School, built around 1890, was the model for a set of schools buildings constructed in the Carman area in the 1890s. Of the four known to have been built, three still survive, although are now used for other purposes.

COUSIN

Another one-room school of this design was Boyne School, built in 1892. Closed in 1930, it was moved and used as a house.

The class photograph of Boyne School, taken in 1894, is a reminder that such facilities provided schooling for all ages, from grade 1 through to grade 12 (if the student was not called away to work in the fields).

Union Point School

COMPARED WITH GARNETT SCHOOL, this school design—carried out for Union Point School District around 1910—is assured and competent, everything you would expect in a public building. What makes this particular example interesting is its design pedigree: it's not every little school that can claim to be the work of one of Manitoba's most important architects.

Before 1900 school facilities were the responsibility of local school boards. Thus, despite the creation of an educational bureaucracy that sought to bring higher standards to school building construction (things like proper heating, lighting, building construction, cleanliness, aesthetics), most one-room schools were of poor quality. A building like Garnett—despite its apparent charm—was certainly a few steps above the norm, but it was the kind of local "adventure" that the authorities were seeking to avoid.

By 1903, with a buoyant economy and better lines of communication, the Department of Education was able to begin a program to upgrade and standardize the quality of rural schools. The Department commissioned a well known Winnipeg architect, Samuel Hooper (later to become the Provincial Architect; see Taché Hall, page 75) to produce three designs that were disseminated to school districts through *The Western School Journal*. It was a turning point. After that, school design and construction adhered to much stricter standards, but in so doing also lost any sense of individuality.

Each of Hooper's schemes addressed a different economic circumstance. The one shown here, "Design for a Frame School Building, No. 3," was for the biggest; the other two designs allowed for more modest budgets. Not surprisingly, Design No. 3 was the least frequently built, and in fact this one, now preserved at St. Joseph, just north of Emerson, is the last of its type remaining.

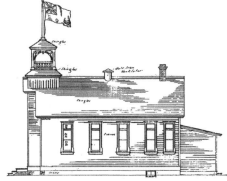

For his "Design for a Frame School Building, No. 3," architect Samuel Hooper created a lively building, with picturesque shape and numerous details.

OTHER OPTIONS

The other two options provided to local school districts by the Department of Education, No. 1 and No. 2, were more modest in their form but still provided necessary amenities and effective designs.

HALLS OF LEARNING

The interior of Union Point School has been carefully preserved as a museum.

Isaac Brock School

WHEN IT WAS BUILT, IN 1913, Isaac Brock School was the biggest school in the province, and cost $248,787 to build. Today that doesn't sound like much.

In the research of buildings the historic costs for materials and services don't have much value. How meaningful is it to know that in 1914 a load of 1 x 8" No. 1 Spruce Shiplap cost $20.50. Or that in 1913 Isaac Brock School cost $248,787? To make those numbers meaningful it is necessary to convert them to contemporary values. To begin to analyze the value of Isaac Brock, factor in the ravages of inflation by finding out how much the value of a dollar has decreased over the years. There is a handy way to do this on the Internet.

The Bank of Canada maintains a Website, with an "Inflation Calculator," (http://www.bank-banque-canada.ca/english/inflation_calc.htm) that provides comparisons of dollar values over the years. Plugging in the numbers for Isaac Brock shows a 1999 dollar value of $4 million.

As a matter for comparison, a new school that went up in Winnipeg in 1997 to replace Greenway School, a slightly smaller version of Isaac Brock, cost $4,560,414. As the French say, *Plus ça change, plus c'est la même chose*. (The more things change, the more they stay the same).

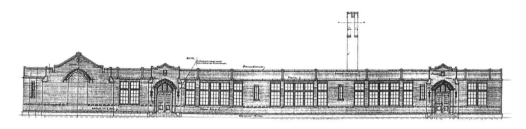

NEW TIMES

The ten-year period when large and ornate schools like Isaac Brock could be built was shattered by World War I and the economic uncertainty that followed. New schools still were required in the 1920s, but these invariably were much smaller. Wolseley School, built in 1921, is a good example of the new type (this drawing is at about the same scale as the one of Isaac Brock). It's low and sleek, providing 13,400 square feet, all on one floor. The new schools, mostly designed by Col. J.N. Semmens, were also subject to a new style: Collegiate Gothic, which featured Gothic detailing (pointed windows and doors) and a new sense of welcoming informality that was a clear conceptual challenge to the grand formality of many pre-War schools.

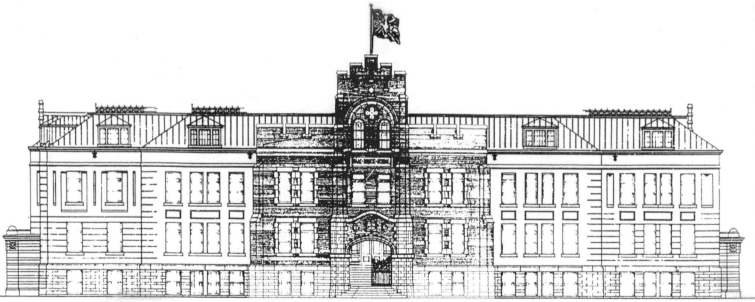

The most impressive period of urban school construction coincided with the province's economic boom in the early 20th century, and between 1907 and 1913 twenty spectacular new schools rose in various Winnipeg neighbourhoods. These schools quickly came to be called palaces. They were big. They were stylistically impressive. And they were expensive. The largest of these was Isaac Brock School, constructed in 1913. These huge buildings, ten of which are still standing, are stately reminders of the wealth, ambition and optimism that defined Winnipeg before the carnage of World War I tarnished everyone's hopes and dreams.

GIMMEE A "B"

Important stories are revealed in some of the details at Isaac Brock. For example this detail, showing one of the school's side entrances conveys the second letter of the alphabet, carved into the mighty stone lintel over the door: a beautiful letter B. It's tempting to think that the B is for "Boys" and that a G on the other side would be for "Girls." But in fact both entrances display the B, presumably for Brock. And what about the type of lettering used? Why is it in Gothic script? The use of Gothic lettering may be delightful, but it was not whimsical. It was, like so much else about the school, a carefully conceived, and not-so-subtle reminder to students of the roots of the prevailing culture: medieval Britain.

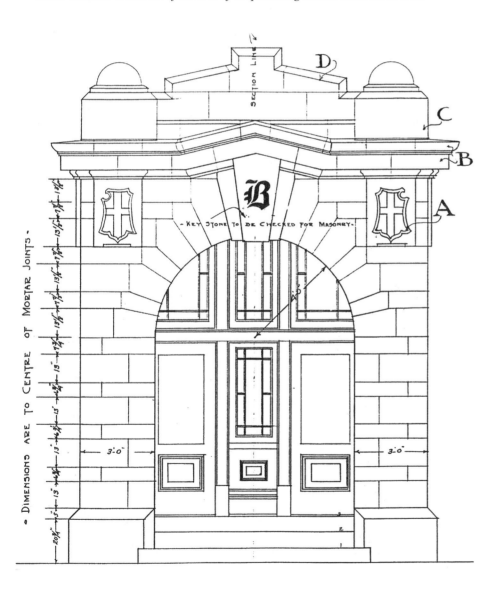

WHAT'S IN A NAME?

Actually, there was quite a bit of contemplation that went on in a school's name choice. The naming of a school has always been ripe with opportunity for those interested in commemorating people, places, history, hopes and dreams. Many Manitoba schools have been named for the geography. Among the most charming: Chicken Hill, Pumpkin Plains, Beautiful Valley, Crocus Hill, Big Woody, Thunder Hill, White Plains, Flowery Bank, Cherry Grove, Picnic Ridge, Sylvan Glade, Teddy Hill. Or as reminders of the Old Country: Londonderry; Aberdeen, Reykjavik, Bukovina, Hoffnungsthal, Antwerpia, Czerona, Finns, Hun's Valley, Champlain. Even abstract concepts and feelings have been enshrined as school names: Utopia, Victory, Happy Thought, Content.

From 1890 to the end of World War I, however, the names, especially of big urban schools in Winnipeg, Brandon and Portage la Prairie, took on a more didactic, even subliminal, role. They became tools in the effort to "Canadianize" the thousands of immigrants arriving in the province almost daily. As little Icelandic, Ukrainian and Polish children arrived at the gates of their new Winnipeg schools, they were met with a pantheon of Canadian (or British) history. Consider this list of all-stars used to name schools in Winnipeg and Brandon before the War: Isaac Brock, Laura Secord, King George V, John King, Earl Grey, Gladstone, Wellington, Somerset, Alexandra, Carlton, Strathcona, Cecil Rhodes, Lord Selkirk, King Edward, Aberdeen, William Whyte, Lord Nelson. Sir Isaac Brock, above (1769-1812), was the hero of Queenston Heights, killed leading his troops against the Americans during the War of 1812.

Brandon College

IN 1991 THE BOARD OF GOVERNORS of Brandon University was faced with a challenge. The two original campus buildings, Brandon College and Clark Hall, were in poor condition. The interiors were especially troubling, with badly sagging floors and supporting joists that were near the end of their structural life. The exteriors were also a problem, with crumbling brickwork and deteriorated window frames. The buildings were also considered fire hazards. Many people felt it was time to replace them with structures that were stylistically modern and also outfitted with every possible contemporary convenience.

The Board, however, never considered tearing down these beloved monuments. The time when such a destructive act was tolerated—the 1950s and 1960s—was past. In this more enlightened age, historic buildings are acknowledged to be the heart of a community and a powerful link to the past.

The answer to the problem was to preserve the exterior walls and the internal Victorian character, while using contemporary construction standards and accommodating modern amenities. The solution was to create a whole new building within the walls of the old. It was an elegant concept that architects Corbett Cibinel of Winnipeg embraced.

The project came in at a cost of $11.3 million. For the architects to carry out their vision, Brandon University looked to traditional and innovative avenues and venues for support. The Brandon College Legacy Campaign raised funds and promotional videos, and computer-generated presentations were also produced and sold. Inspired when workers found old materials in the walls, people were invited, for $10, to sign the underside of cedar roof shingles, preserving for posterity their contribution to the city's heritage.

The resulting complex is a monument to new and old. Architect George Cibinel of Corbett Cibinel put it best, responding to suggestions that the restoration costs were extravagant and that the buildings should have been demolished: "We spent an additional seven per cent to add the level of quality and details. I've never regretted putting an extra seven per cent effort into any of my work."

The first building at Brandon University, called Brandon College (now the Administration Building) was built in 1901 to designs by Hugh McCowan of Winnipeg and served as a dormitory for 70 young men. In 1906 veteran Brandon architect W.A. Elliott designed a Women's Residence, Clark Hall. Both buildings were conceived in the then-popular Romanesque Revival style, which was characterized by blocky massing, groupings of round-arched windows and attention to the possibilities of brick detailing, seen here in belt courses encircling the buildings and highlighting the window heads and corbel tables (stepped brick courses at the roof line). The buildings, together, have been designated by the province as heritage sites.

DANGEROUS ANGLE

All of the construction work at Brandon University involved careful attention to original building fabric, and the replication where possible of features and details. One particularly challenging aspect of the work involved an attempt to shore up, and save, the tower of Clark Hall. In order to remove the original deteriorated brick and rooted beams beneath it, construction crews had first to prop up the tower on steel I-beams that were slid at an angle under the sloping lower edges. For several months, as work progressed, Brandon citizens were treated to a wonder of engineering, as the tower appeared to hang precariously in mid-air.

The building is named for Archbishop Antoine Tache, Archbishop of St. Boniface and second rector of St. Boniface College, an affiliate of the Roman Catholic Church. In 1877, that college, established in 1854, was joined with St. John's College (Anglican, formed in 1866) and Manitoba College (Presbyterian, established in 1871) to form the first provincial university.

PROVINCIAL ARCHITECTS

The architects who designed Tache Hall, Samuel Hooper and Victor Horwood, were responsible for many of the public government buildings erected for the provincial government between 1904 and 1915, most of which still stand in Manitoba. Both men were Englishmen who immigrated to Ontario with their parents (Hooper in 1869, Horwood in 1884). Hooper (1851-1911), had trained as a stonemason and in Winnipeg was well known for stone monument designs. He returned to London to study architecture and after a successful career back in Winnipeg was appointed Manitoba's first Provincial Architect in 1904. That position required the incumbent and his staff (of about 30, including his assistant, Victor Horwood) to design new government buildings required by the growing province. The office's output was impressive, with more than 30 major buildings produced (court houses, land titles offices, power plants, normal schools, colleges, mental health centres). Hooper died in 1911 and Horwood (1878-1939) was appointed the new Provincial Architect. In many cases he carried out designs already completed under Hooper's reign. Horwood alone prepared the design programme for the Legislative Building Competition. The scandal that dogged the building of the Legislature (see page 44) brought Horwood into disgrace. He retired from practice, and the office of the Provincial Architect was disbanded several years later.

Tache Hall

A BUILDING WHOSE FAÇADE IS 185 metres long—almost the length of two football fields—requires an architect with special design skills. A successful solution would entail the creation of a wall that is, at one level, simple and harmonious—with a clear hierarchy of entrances and internal functions—and on another level is rewarding to look at—with a surface that is interesting and even challenging—and thus appealing to the eye.

This kind of design attitude was brought to bear on the design of Tache Hall, the main dormitory at the University of Manitoba, built in 1911-12, and one of the longest "walls" in Manitoba.

Looking at the building as a whole, it is possible to imagine the design team, Provincial Architect Samuel Hooper and his assistant Victor Horwood, at work. They simplified their task by first dividing the building into two identical sections. This decision reflected the design programme, which required a main entrance block and two flanking dormitories, one for women, the other for men. The simple symmetry enabled Hooper and Horwood to focus their energies on just half the resulting building, at 90 metres long and almost 15 metres high—an area of 1,350 square metres—still a formidable challenge.

It is not known what ideas may have floated around the Provincial Architect's office regarding style, the most important decision that affects all other choices. What is known, is that the result is a delightfully eclectic expression combining Georgian Revival with Tudor Gothic. Maybe everyone in the office had a say.

The Georgian Revival was the choice for the overall form and then for the walls, seen here as expanses of red brick contrasted with crisp white details in limestone. The primary form borrowed here was the gable shape. And it was used with abandon, as dormer windows in the roof itself, and then in the four slightly projecting bays with their tall false fronts inscribed with stone details in the shape of gables. A wealth of classical elements and details were explored to enrich the surface: Italian Baroque volutes, Tuscan columns, broken pediments, quoins (the snaggle-toothed detail at many of the corners). Tudor Gothic, with a *soupçon* of Dutch Colonial, was employed at the roof.

A review of the dozens of buildings that Hooper and Horwood designed suggests that they were capable, but not necessarily inspired, architects. Tache Hall, however, appears to have stretched the team to reach a high level of excellence. It is sophisticated, stately and elegant. It might even be thought of as Hooper's masterpiece, an authoritative statement about his design skills and architectural knowledge.

Lost Treasures — Schools

The loss of historic schools was one of the most troublesome consequences of school consolidation movements, especially of the 1950s and 60s. Particularly heartbreaking is the absence of the big schools that once stood in nearly every Manitoba town. Even in Winnipeg, where the preservation of larger schools was more feasible, there have been troubling losses. The images on these pages suggest the extent of the loss—these were certainly amongst the finest buildings to grace our communities. Gone forever.

Central School, Winnipeg, built in 1882 and designed by James Chisholm. Almost literally topped with a crown, the school once stood behind St. Mary's Roman Catholic Cathedral in Winnipeg and is a fine example of Italianate design influences.

Morden Collegiate, built in 1894. A ruggedly handsome building of local fieldstone, with a flamboyant roof. The small windows in the large school, like those of so many others, caused lighting challenges inside.

Manitoba College, Winnipeg, designed by renowned early Winnipeg architect C.A. Barber, the building stood at the end of Vaughan Street, on Ellice Avenue and was an eclectic mix of details, making it a building like no other.

Two Killarney Schools, one from 1893, left, the other built in 1906, featured prominent bell towers.

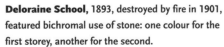

Deloraine School, 1893, destroyed by fire in 1901, featured bichromal use of stone: one colour for the first storey, another for the second.

Chapter 6

6

COMMERCIAL

Hudson's Bay Company Store

WHEN YOU'VE BEEN AROUND for more than 300 years, like the Hudson's Bay Company has, you learn to adapt in order to survive.

The company is the oldest commercial enterprise in Canada, inaugurated in 1670 as "The Governor and Company of Adventurers Trading into Hudson Bay." Its royal charter, granted by King Charles II of England, established a huge fur-trading territory called Rupert's Land (comprising much of western Canada), named for the king's cousin and one of the original key shareholders, Prince Rupert.

The company was a highly lucrative venture, providing furs for the fashion industry in Europe. Its enterprise was not without competition, however, and beginning in 1763 the Hudson's Bay Company (HBC) was entangled in a bitter struggle with the North West Company of Montreal for supremacy in the fur trade. The battle ended with their amalgamation in 1821 under the aegis of the Hudson's Bay Company.

The days of the company's dominion were numbered. The arrival of the Selkirk Settlers in 1812 at Red River, was the first sign of changing times. By 1850 the success of settlers' farming operations, the gradual population growth in the West, and the decline of the fur trade itself, impelled HBC officials to consider other economic opportunities. When the company sold Rupert's Land to Canada in 1869, it focused its efforts on the retail trade and land speculation.

For its first foray into Winnipeg's retail community, in 1882, the company relied on a reliable architectural convention of the day.

In his design for the new HBC department store in Winnipeg, architect Ernest Barott of Toronto followed clear directions from the company and created a palace of commerce. Like a Renaissance palace, the building was a carefully composed box, enlivened with Classical details like pilasters (flattened columns set against a wall), Corinthian capitals (the decorative work atop the pilasters), a deep cornice and a balustrade at the roof line. The whole building was carried out in local Tyndall stone cladding.

FIRST TIME

When it was built, in 1882, the original HBC store on Main Street in Winnipeg was a completely up-to-date store, combining a multitude of "departmental" goods, a restaurant, and on the southwest corner, a candy factory. The façade design was a winner, with arched openings. Piers and decorative brickwork at the roof line combined to create a highly animated surface. Each of the three doors seen in this old photograph was highlighted with a crisply detailed pediment (the triangular section above the door) and flanking columns. The ancient Classical motif, originally denoting a spiritual space, became an inviting entrance into a luscious world of commerce. This building was demolished in 1932, seven years after the new Hudson's Bay Store opened on Portage Avenue.

EATON'S

The Eaton's Store on Portage Avenue in Winnipeg was, at its construction in 1905, completely modern. The warehouse effect, with utilitarian bands of windows and unrelieved brick work was a conscious aesthetic decision intended to convey to shoppers the no-frills, no-nonsense, but also trustworthy, character of the store's founder Timothy Eaton. The style was an obvious alternative to that embraced by the Bay 20 years later, which conveyed a much more expensive impression. The Eaton's store was closed in 1999.

The building was a highly decorated Italianate design, not markedly different from other such operations along Main Street (at that time the city's busiest commercial thoroughfare). But its location, at the corner of Main and York, allowed the company to create two major facades along each street, and thus to produce a greater physical presence than its competitors.

To make it even more popular, the operation was a "departmental" store, a kind of operation introduced in France in the early 19th century, and one that had become very popular in North America, offering customers the opportunity to buy a variety of goods in one convenient stop.

The Bay's retail operation was a success. However, on the horizon was lurking a formidable competitor, an opponent that posed as great a threat as the old North West Company had in the early 19th century. Eaton's, the retail behemoth from the East, had been eyeing Winnipeg for some time, and in 1905 began construction on a gigantic store on Portage Avenue. The new building immediately eclipsed all other retailers in the city. It was huge, measuring 95 by 137 metres and offered an impressive variety of services.

The Hudson's Bay Company finally responded in 1925 to Eaton's challenge with its own fabulous new building on Portage Avenue. In contrast to Eaton's severe warehouse aesthetic, the Board of Directors at The Hudson's Bay Company decided that a more elegant, expensive-looking building would not only create a suitable image, but also would establish a clear competitive alternative to Eaton's. In fact, the Company built three other magnificent emporiums in major western cities besides Winnipeg: Calgary (1912), Vancouver (1914-16) and Victoria (1914-21).

In 1999 the venerable Eaton's Company was dissolved and its stores closed. The HBC remains, as it has for 300 years.

Winnipeg CPR Station

IT'S IRONIC THAT ONE OF THE MOST important symbols of Manitoba's settlement era, the grand Canadian Pacific Railway Station on Higgins Avenue in Winnipeg, is now used by representatives of the very people those settlers often displaced, the Aboriginal peoples of Manitoba.

Winnipeg's early history was strongly shaped by two corporate interests – the Hudson's Bay Company (HBC) and the Canadian Pacific Railway (CPR). Prior to 1870 it was the HBC and the associated Red River Settlement that established the city's location, basic patterns of growth and economy. The arrival of the CPR in 1881 confirmed Winnipeg's place as the dominant transportation and marketing centre on the Prairies, at least during the region's formative years up to 1910. The route of the main rail line into Winnipeg—through the city's original site of settlement, Point Douglas—and the location of a station near Main Street also affected the course of urban development.

With hundreds of thousands immigrants passing through the doors of successive stations, including this one, built in 1904-05, the CPR station became the focus for commercial and retail activity, as well as for the necessary government buildings required to process all the newcomers.

The station also came to symbolize the power and prosperity of the province. At its peak 17 trains unloaded passengers every day. The decline of rail travel in the 1950s and the closing of the adjacent Royal Alexandra Hotel in late 1960s (see Lost Treasures, page 115) could have doomed the station, but the determination and foresight of the Aboriginal Council of Manitoba has ensured that this remarkable Manitoba landmark was saved, and rehabilitated.

Designed by Edward and William Maxwell of Montreal, Winnipeg's CPR Station is a transcendent example of Beaux-Arts Classical design. Built of Wisconsin red brick and light grey Tyndall stone, the building reflected pomp and circumstance.

UNION STATION

The two other companies that competed with the CPR for more than two decades, Canadian Northern and Grand Trunk Pacific, joined forces in 1909 to build their own grand Winnipeg station. Set impressively on Main Street at the foot of Broadway, the building was a stark contrast to the CPR's exuberant presence on Higgins Avenue. New York architects Warren and Wetmore, who had designed Grand Central Station in New York, produced a building as imposing and impressive as the CPR's, using however a more severe aesthetic, with clean crisp surfaces of Manitoba limestone.

WINNIPEG WINS

The location of the CPR mainline through Winnipeg was not a sure thing. The company's superintendent of engineering, Sandford Fleming, proposed a more obvious route north of Winnipeg, passing through Selkirk. Winnipeg business interests couldn't believe it. To persuade the CPR they offered the company a bonus of $300,000 to build a bridge over the Red River and agreed to provide land for a station and perpetual exemption from taxes. In 1881 the first CPR train crossed the new Louise Street Bridge.

Dauphin CN Station

This old photograph, from around 1945, shows the handsome Canadian Northern Railway station in Dauphin on the right. The town hall is pictured on the left. Stretching between them, along the tracks, is a carefully manicured lawn, with ornamental shrubs and flowers. For many years it was a beloved spot, where townsfolk enjoyed a stroll in the warm afternoon sun and the fragrant smell of lilacs.

RAILWAY SERVICE WAS ESSENTIAL as Manitoba was opened to settlement and agricultural commerce during the 1880s and 1890s. In one of the province's greatest waves of construction, first the Canadian Pacific Railway (CPR), and then other smaller companies, laid down hundreds of kilometres of track and built scores of station buildings. In 1896, a fledgling railway, the Lake Manitoba Railway and Canal Company, was completed from Gladstone to Dauphin. This stretch of track became the genesis for a major transcontinental service. The company, renamed Canadian Northern in 1899 (part of the Canadian National system in 1920), eventually came to rival the mighty CPR. Dauphin was one of Canadian Northern's most important divisional points. The station, built in 1912, was among Manitoba's finest pieces of railway architecture, with its impressive size, picturesque roofline, dormers, turrets and decorative brick and stone work.

Railway stations were intended through placement and design to make a powerful statement about their place in the local economy and in the community. Thus they were often situated at the centre of town, strategically placed at the terminus of a main street.

There were other aspects to the operation of the railway station. For one thing, many stations also were the homes of the station master and his family, provided with living quarters in a second storey apartment. For some station masters there was an interest in producing decorative gardens that lay adjacent to the station. For many pioneer communities the railway garden was an oasis of green in an otherwise dusty, mud-caked commercial core. The gardens at the Dauphin station were amongst the best in the province.

A LONG, LONG WAY

This photograph eloquently sums up two important aspects of railway station architecture. First, the building is inordinately long. And for good reason. The length ensured access to the railway cars from various points, both for passengers waiting under the sweeping roof but also for those areas of the building devoted to storage. Secondly, the building's high level of design quality is showcased here. Only Union Station in Winnipeg outranked Dauphin in terms of importance in Canadian Northern's Manitoba system. The building's fortress-like quality, with turrets, corner tower block and a crescendo of the forms rising to the central peak made it a memorable and impressive focus at Dauphin's core.

TEA AMID THE CINDERS

Train stations of the early 20th century are seldom associated with tea and crumpets. But for those locations where the rail company and an obliging agent took the time, small parks and gardens were important green spaces. This recollection of a station garden, from Hamiota: Grains of the Century, *provides insight into social stratification at the turn of the century:*

"On the east side of the station house was a small enclosure of well kept grass and shade trees. This small park was used during the summer months for special social teas among the town's so-called elite. Strawberry teas were the highlight of the late spring season. To the west of the station alongside the loading platform was a larger enclosure of green grass and trees. Here the general public gathered during the summer when the town band was in attendance, or a visiting group of Salvation Army people held an open-air meeting."

Tergesen's General Store

THE TWO OLDEST RETAIL ESTABLISHMENTS in Manitoba—the Hudson's Bay Company (HBC) and the North West Company—can trace their origins back several centuries; the HBC to 1670, the NWC to 1776. The retail operation that claims third spot on the roster of longest-lived businesses—H.P. Tergesen and Sons General Store in Gimli—recently celebrated its first century.

That impressive claim underlines the tenacity of the Tergesens, and also points to the fragility of retail operations. There have been hundreds, even thousands, of small commercial enterprises that have served Manitoba. That none except Tergesen's has survived a century, and that few have even weathered 50 years, is worth pondering. The enduring success of the Tergesen Store can be attributed to a combination of hard work and good luck. It started out well, with a good foundation.

When Hans Pjetur Tergesen arrived in Gimli, via Saskatchewan, in 1899, he quickly established a hardware business and built a small store. With training as a tinsmith, he manufactured and sold pots, pans, oil cans and stove pipes. At first the family lived over the store, but additions carried out in 1912-13, including a second storey (removed in the 1920s), compelled them to move. The larger store also featured an ice cream parlour and drugstore.

Over the years the Tergesen Store adapted to changing circumstances and became a Gimli institution. It was not just a popular shopping destination, it was also a focus for community gatherings. It accommodated school classrooms and served occasionally as a community hall for plays and dances. The loyalty of customers, a shrewd focus on Icelandic culture and the popularity of Gimli as a resort community have ensured that Tergesen's is still alive and kicking.

Built in 1899 by a local man, Jon Bjornson, the Tergesen Store was architecturally typical of commercial enterprises of the day. While it has some modest pretensions—a broad cornice and brackets—it was otherwise utilitarian, with all the focus going to the two doors and the adjacent expanses of display windows. There was one interesting innovation that Hans Tergesen chose for the building: the exterior walls were clad with metal panels, pressed to resemble brick. Given his background as a tinsmith, that material might have appealed to him on a personal level, and probably also was seen as a novelty that would help promote his store.

While this photograph of the interior of the Tergesen Store is from 1915, it could just as well have been taken yesterday. The store has been lovingly preserved through the years and is largely intact, with original pressed tin ceiling and walls, hardwood floors, oak and glass shelving units, display cases and light fixtures throughout.

THE LANDRY GENERAL STORE

While the Tergesen Store was typical of small retail concerns from the turn of the century, the Landry General Store in Mariapolis, 150 kilometres southeast of Brandon, certainly was not. Looking for all the world like a major train station, the store defies belief. In a community that contains no more than a few hundred buildings, its size and architectural character suggest the ambitions and hopes for growth that must have imbued its first proprietor Calixte Landry when he built the establishment in 1914.

Birks Building

Architects Percy Nobbs and his partner George Hyde, assisted in some of the detail work by friend Ramsay Traquair, brought considerable attention to bear on their project for the wealthy Birks Brothers, and created a magnificent Renaissance palace in the heart of Winnipeg.

JUST THROUGH THEIR FORM and in their details, many buildings impart powerful stories of their purpose and history. The former Birks Building, in Winnipeg, told its story much more literally, not just through its style, but also through sculptures and paintings that reminded and instructed passers-by about their business: jewelry. Like the little blue box that became a company trademark, the building at the corner of Portage Avenue and Smith Street was to become an important landmark in the city.

The building was actually constructed for the Young Men's Christian Association in 1900-01, but within twelve years was already inadequate for the Association's needs. Henry Birks and Sons of Montreal, which had established a jewelry shop on Main Street in 1903, was eager to move onto the newly prospering Portage Avenue. The old "Y" was a perfect fit, at least in terms of location and size. The interior arrangements naturally would have to be completely altered. But Birks also concluded that the exterior architectural character had to be transformed. For this work they called on Percy Nobbs, the former head of the School of Architecture at Montreal's McGill University.

Mr. Nobbs' renovation, carried out in 1914, obliterated the slightly eccentric building designed by George Browne of Winnipeg. In its place stood a sumptuous Italian Renaissance palace. Nobbs' building was derived in theory from the 16th century houses of Florence and Rome, in which plain stucco surfaces allowed for an emphasis on window treatments and on the potential for grand architectural statement at the roofline. In the academic circles in which Nobbs circulated, this particular version of the Renaissance Revival style was called astylar, to distinguish it from another popular Renaissance Revival strain characterized by the use of columns. The astylar strain was a perfect choice for Birks' needs, allowing for the integration on the façade of the richly sculpted medallions and magnificently detailed frieze that spoke of the history of jewels and of the jewelry business.

Today's owner Brian Finnegan, and architects Cohlmeyer Associates, were diligent in researching the building's original character, and ensured that Percy Nobbs' salmon-orange stucco colouring was restored. Such attention to detail has made the old Birks Building not only one of the most visible "new" buildings on Portage Avenue, but can also be seen as a major vote of confidence in the viability of downtown Winnipeg.

IT'S FUN TO STAY AT THE YMCA

Before becoming a symbol of conspicuous wealth and sumptuous comfort, the Birks Building was better known to Winnipeggers as a place to sweat and play. From its construction in 1900 to its sale in 1912 to Birks, the building was home to the city's Young Men's Christian Association, the YMCA. Comparing this photograph, from around 1905, to the one above, shows the incredible transformation that all but effaced the original building. The old building's fenestration and massing were retained, but the whole thing was gussied-up in a new set of clothes, these ones from the Renaissance.

IF WALLS COULD TALK

Bank of Montreal

THE OLD STORY GOES THAT when asked why he robbed banks, famed hold-up artist Willie Sutton replied, "Because that's where the money is." It's a charming and apparently naïve answer that cuts to the heart of the matter. Had Mr. Sutton been an architectural historian, he might have responded in a similarly insouciant way if asked why bank buildings were such obvious displays of conspicuous wealth, "Because banks are made of money."

The Bank of Montreal in Winnipeg, built in 1913, is just such a building. The bank, and its architects, the famed New York firm of McKim, Mead and White, used every trick in the book to create one of the most impressive buildings in the province. The site—at the historic and strategic corner of Portage Avenue and Main Street—and the style—a veritable Roman temple in its purest form—were just the first, albeit vital, orders of business. It was in the choice of materials, expensive materials—like Botticino marble from Northern Italy; white granite quarried at Bethel, Vermont; brass for the teller's grilles; copper for the roofs; white oak for the woodwork; and gold leaf for the ceilings of the banking hall—that the real wealth of the company was put on display. At a widely advertised cost of $1,295,000, it was sure to impress even the most unsophisticated of visitors to the bank. It surely would have rattled the famous character created in Stephen Leacock's short story, *My Financial Career*: "When I go into a bank I get rattled. The clerks rattle me; the wickets rattle me; the sight of the money rattles me; everything rattles me." And surely the one million dollars worth of gold leaf on the ceiling would have rattled him.

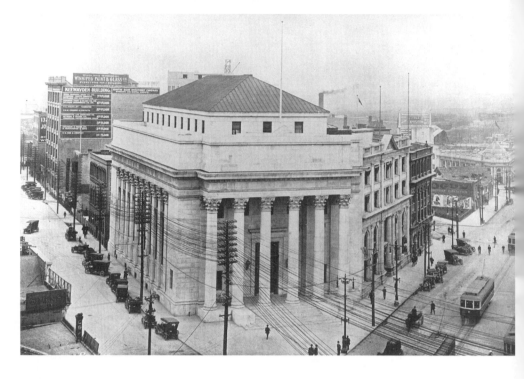

America's leading proponents and interpreters of the classical architecture of Greece and Rome, the New York firm of McKim, Mead and White, designed for the Bank of Montreal a conservative building. It was a perfect expression of the bank's corporate identity. To mark their 100th anniversary in Winnipeg, in 1976 the bank undertook a major refurbishment, and in the late 1990s opened the historic banking hall after having vacated it for several years.

SEVERE BUT SUMPTUOUS

The building may have been architecturally severe, with little applied ornament, but it wasn't modest. And once inside, the clientele was engulfed in a banking hall that was at once impressive and tasteful, an exquisite example of neo-classical design. The vestibule was finished with Botticino marble from Northern Italy. The banking hall itself was majestic, measuring 47 by 28 metres and with a soaring 20-metre ceiling. Patrons tread over marble floors while admiring the ceiling, finished in gold leaf. An Ionic colonnade encircled the banking hall and opened into a mezzanine floor. The two top storeys of the building were reserved for living quarters for bank employees, and the third floor contained a dining room and lounge facilities. One storey above this, bank officials maintained sleeping quarters, a long row of bedrooms that boasted sitting rooms and clothing closets, and which were punctuated with bathrooms at various points.

The Northern Bank

The bank incorporated circular medallions, called tondos, inset with sculpted bison heads to affiliate it with the symbol of the province.

THERE ONCE WERE DOZENS OF BANK COMPANIES operating in Manitoba. Big eastern institutions had moved into Manitoba in the late 19th century following the province's dramatic growth. Banks that still exist, like the Bank of Montreal and the Bank of Nova Scotia, were joined by operations that either went out of business or were amalgamated into larger entities: The Bank of Hamilton, Traders Bank, Commercial Bank of Manitoba, Dominion Bank, Bank of Hamilton, Bank of Hochelaga, Northern Crown Bank, Ontario Bank, Bank of Ottawa, Merchant's Bank.

There were also a number of private banks that provided services. One of these concerns, The Northern Bank, was opened by A.W. Law and Company in Melita in 1898. The bank was taken over by the Union Bank, which itself was amalgamated with the Royal Bank.

Architecturally, The Northern Bank was one of the most interesting small bank designs in Manitoba. Befitting its function, it was a brick and stone creation, solid and comforting. It was also designed with a medley of traditional Classical details understood to convey to patrons a sense of stability—Doric columns supporting a broad entablature and cornice, a keystone in the broad arch carved with wandering grooves (known technically as a vermiculated surface), and an entrance created with a Greek-temple pediment and, on the pilasters, elegant scrolls.

HEIST!

On a Saturday morning in late September 1910, the village of Melita, and The Northern Bank, were in for a big, big surprise.

Bandits from the United States arrived in the early morning hours, their first stop being the town's power station, where they bound and gagged the night engineer to prevent him from turning on the street lights. They then moved on to the bank, broke the door down, and proceeded to work on the vault with a hammer and chisel. Bank employees living upstairs were awakened by the racket and when they confronted the robbers were escorted out and guarded.

Eight charges were laid on the vault, and each was detonated, providing access to the vault's contents: $7,700 and $90,000 in securities. Town resident Walter Waite was awakened by the explosions and made his way to the town fire bell, which was vigorously rung, bringing out many townsfolk. The first on the scene was Reverend Thomas Beveridge, who encountered gunfire, with one shot wounding him in the foot. After the haul the bank robbers made their escape back to the United States and were never identified or caught.

REAL MONEY

As late as the 1950s banks could create and use their own bank notes.

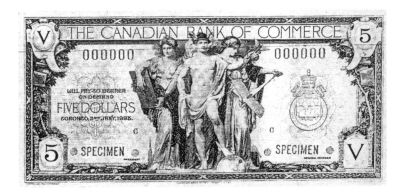

Wawanesa Insurance Building

IF IT WASN'T ASSOCIATED WITH ONE OF Manitoba's great business success stories, one might pass right by this modest yellow brick building in Wawanesa. But because it was the first formal home of the Wawanesa Mutual Insurance Company, it is hard to ignore. Some people even make a pilgrimage here to see from whence an empire grew.

The Wawanesa Mutual Insurance Company was created in 1896, the brainchild of Alonzo Fowler Kempton. The idea apparently came to him while on the road selling fire insurance. Supposedly camped on the prairies with his friend, Charles Kerr, and enjoying a glass of whiskey, Kempton laid out a plan. Recognizing that the available insurance provided by eastern concerns was expensive and inflexible to farmers' needs, he proposed that farmers form their own insurance company, one that charged lower premiums than a regular Insurance Board company.

Encouraged by Kerr, he first made his pitch in Glenboro, where he was rebuffed for his reputation as a drinker. Farmers in the Wawanesa area were apparently more tolerant and Wawanesa Mutual began its operation in October of 1896 by insuring straw-burning threshing machines. Over the years the company has grown to become the second largest Canadian-owned insurance company in the country.

The Mutual's first office was located in a second-storey room over the local drugstore. In 1901 the company was able to move to its own building, a solid brick structure without unnecessary detail. That building was vacated for new quarters across the street in 1930, but the original company home has been preserved and today houses the collection of the Sipiweske Museum.

The old Wawanesa Insurance Company Building from 1901 was like many small commercial buildings of the age—unremarkable. Some modest attempts at architectural pretension, with the disposition of bricks, made it slightly more interesting to look at but in the end it was, like the threshing machines the company built its early reputation on, simple and straightforward.

ALONZO FOWLER KEMPTON (1863-1939)

The founder of the Wawanesa Insurance Company was larger-than-life, a born entrepreneur and salesman. Alonzo Fowler, seen beside the driver in this photograph, came to Manitoba from Nova Scotia with his parents in 1881, and began his career here selling household goods to new immigrants. Besides his great legacy, The Wawanesa, he also ventured into stock insurance. He formed the Wawanesa Wagon Seat Company, which manufactured a more comfortable wagon seat, and created the Canada Hone Company to make leather razor strops. Kempton was renowned for his hearty appetites and the need for grand display. He had the biggest house and the finest car in town. And he was a formidable drinker, a pursuit that may have had a part in his downfall. During a stormy meeting of The Wawanesa's Board of Directors in 1922 he offered his resignation, and probably to his great surprise, it was accepted. Kempton moved to Vernon, British Columbia and died penniless in 1939.

Electric Railway Chambers

PRODUCTS AND SERVICES MARKETING are a pervasive part of late 20th-century life. Today we live with, and even block out, standard marketing devices including billboards, busboards, print, radio, television and Internet advertising. In 1913, however, few of these mediums existed and so it took marketing ingenuity to hatch the idea of using the very fabric of a building not just to command attention from passersby, as many buildings do with their sheer size or style, but advertise and demonstrate their new product.

By day, the Electric Railway Chambers Building was another skyscraper in Winnipeg's downtown. There is no doubt it grabbed the public's attention. Architects Ralph Pratt and Donald Ross, with the help of Chicago-based architect Charles Frost, made sure of that with their terrific eleven-storey design, executed in the Italian Renaissance style. It featured an imposing façade comprised of polished granite and terra cotta, laced in a multitude of details including embossed shields, an ornate cornice, and full-bodied lions seated with their heads looking towards the terrain below. Exotically-detailed columns stretch from the bottom of the building to its top where they are crowned by round arches. Altogether the effect creates a magnificent architectural presence near the corner of Portage Avenue and Main Street, on Notre Dame Avenue.

To this day, the Electric Railway Chambers adds to its power when strings of clear lights, designed as an integral part of the building, outline the columns and the arches when turned on. The lights, lovely in their glow and symmetry rise high in the Exchange District and create an ethereal presence in the night sky. Years ago, when almost every other building downtown was cloaked in darkness, and otherwise invisible at night, the dramatic light show at the Electric Railway Chambers must have attracted constant comment and been a memorable sight.

What better way for the Winnipeg Electric Railway to advertise its new products and services. The Winnipeg Electric Railway operated the city's electric streetcar system and its first hydro-electric utility from 1895 to 1953. The building's presence just around the corner from historic Portage and Main, and the dramatic display of rising and arching lights, perfectly showcased to Winnipeggers and visitors the allure of electricity and new-fangled light bulbs. This demonstration of lights, alongside a majestic new building, was an impressive marketing display.

ELECTRIC RAILWAY BUILDING WINNIPEG.

During the day you would hardly know that the Electric Railway Chambers Building contains 6,000 light bulbs inset in decorative pockets lining the exterior columns, and secured and wired in place. The lights are illuminated in a timed sequence, beginning with the bottom storeys so that the display is even more captivating.

ELECTRIC RAILWAY BUILDING WINNIPEG.

Union Bank Tower

BUILT BY DARLING AND PEARSON, a Toronto company famed for such Canadian landmarks as the Sun Life Assurance Company Building in Montreal and The Royal Ontario Museum in Toronto, the Union Bank Tower, located at William Avenue and Main Street in Winnipeg, was Manitoba's first skyscraper. Darling and Pearson created the metaphor that Canadian financial institutions of the day sought, that of towering strength, through a sure hand for style and creative use of opulent materials and details. Its social and structural significance is illuminated in a series of images, all of which capture defining moments from Winnipeg's past.

THE BANK'S WAY

This is the first presentation drawing of Winnipeg's Union Bank Tower by Darling and Pearson. The Bank's choice to commission the company to design the tower publicly conveyed its wealth and sophistication. The building is timeless and impressive, a worthy addition, then and now, to the firm's roster of Canadian architectural successes. The Bank paid dearly for Darling and Pearson's services and vision, coughing up $420,000 in 1903, the equivalent of approximately $10 million in 2000.

This first presentation drawing is a treasured historical record, and demonstrates the kinds of changes that often affect architectural projects as they progress from original concept to final construction. The top floors envisioned here are heavily articulated, rich with ornament and height, the crowning glory to master design. But along the way, someone changed their mind. In a photograph of the building, to the right, the floor is simpler, and presumably, a less costly version.

The new steel frame technology not only made for a lighter-weight, fire resistant building, it also allowed for the creation of a taller building. The Union Bank Tower, at 10 storeys, was the tallest building in Winnipeg when it was constructed and towered over neighbouring structures. Where other downtown buildings were seldom more than four storeys high (approximately the limit possible with standard brick construction), this one inaugurated to Winnipeg the age of the skyscraper.

NEW TECHNOLOGY

Until the construction of the Union Bank Tower in 1903-04, large-scale commercial buildings in Manitoba were constructed of bricks which created solid weight-bearing walls. They were, in a word, heavy. But Darling and Pearson, and the building contractor George Fuller Company of New York, introduced Winnipeg to a then, new-fangled material, steel; and entirely new construction technique, steel frame.

Steel frame construction was gaining wide acceptance in eastern regions of Canada and the United States. It was revolutionary in changing forever the architectural landscape. Winnipeggers must have been fascinated, if not somewhat frightened to gaze up at the building evolving before their eyes. "How," they might have thought, "is it possible that the intermediate or middle floors of the tower have been completed, while the rest of the building, specifically the lower floors are a mere steel skeleton, open to the elements?" Even today, the technique appears to defy gravity, and common sense.

HISTORIC BACKDROP

As a background to the crowds gathered to voice their dissent in the Winnipeg General Strike of 1919, the Union Bank Tower looms large. This photograph captures the moment just before police stormed the strikers gathered on Main Street. The result of that violet confrontation—called Bloody Sunday—was the collapse of the strike and the imprisonment of labour leaders. Symbolically, the Bank and the strikers who pressed up against it are forever linked. For the Union Bank Tower, with all of its wealth and omnipotence, represented many of the things the striker's of the day opposed.

Today the Union Bank Tower is more commonly known as the Royal Bank Tower, but is no longer a functioning banking outlet.

Lost Treasures — Commercial Buildings

Whether claimed individually by fire, the need to improve or adapt a business opportunity, or taken wholus-bolus in more recent massive development projects, the losses of commercial buildings is unsettling. For those removed decades ago, history lovers can only mull over old photographs and lament that there have been so few survivors.

THE CITY MARKET, WINNIPEG.

Market Building, Winnipeg, 1897. In retrospect one of the great losses to the city, along with City Hall, the market building was removed in 1964 to make way for a new civic complex.

Bailey Block, Portage la Prairie, 1901. Once a striking presence on Saskatchewan Avenue, with its distinctive corner turret, the block was lost to fire in the early 1990's.

The **Alexandria Block** in Emerson, from the early 1880s, was a building of impressive length that was demolished years ago.

The west side of **Main Street,** north of Portage Avenue, as seen around 1910. All of the exuberant stone and brick buildings visible here have been lost to development.

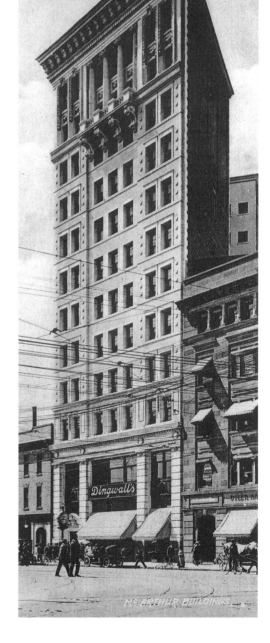

Better known as the **Childs Building,** the tall and elegant McArthur Building was demolished to make way for the new Toronto-Dominion Tower.

Palace Stables, Winnipeg, 1882. With the demise of the horse as the primary source of transportation, a whole set of buildings was also lost, like this Italianate-style stable that once stood on Smith Street near Graham Avenue.

Chapter 7

INDUSTRIAL

7

Inglis Grain Elevators

IN RETROSPECT, THE FORM OF the traditional prairie grain elevator seems inevitable. Just make a tall box, and to protect the top of the internal elevator mechanism add a small gabled "hat." But when the first commercial grain elevator was constructed in Manitoba, at Niverville, in 1878, the form was altogether different, an elegant cylinder with a delightful cupola at the top. Quickly, however, the more familiar shape was introduced, and so was born what has become a prairie icon, the West's great architectural symbol.

A grain elevator is a model of simplicity and efficiency. The whole thing revolves around the elevator, a continuous vertical belt outfitted with metal or wooden cups to hold the grain. The cups on the belt are oriented to pick up grain deposited into a pit at the bottom of the building and raise it to the top, the head, where it is distributed via a system of ducts to one of the bins arrayed around the building's perimeter.

At the industry's height, in 1911, there were 707 grain elevators in Manitoba. Nearly every community had one, and bigger centres typically featured a whole row, lined up like brooding sentinels on the local rail line.

For all their visual power—simple, elemental shapes and enormous size—and their obvious usefulness, the traditional grain elevator has succumbed to the forces of changing technology and shifts in the farming economy. They are quickly being replaced by huge concrete facilities. There are nevertheless still about 200 traditional grain elevators in service in this province. But there is only one elevator "line" still standing, in Inglis (about 140 kilometres west of Dauphin), a rare reminder of what was once a ubiquitous part of our architectural past.

The elevators at Inglis have been recognized as sites of federal importance, and by the province as protected heritage sites. An ambitious restoration and rehabilitation project will eventually see the complex become a centre for the interpretation of the industry and of elevator technology. One of the old buildings is currently being restored, with all the interior workings made accessible so that visitors can get up close to the business end of one of the most important buildings of this province's past.

The line of five elevators at Inglis, all built during the 1920s, is the best remaining example of an elevator line in Canada. The group not only represents architecturally and mechanically intact buildings, but the collection also combines at one place several of the important companies that controlled the grain trade. In 1996 the line was declared a site of national historic significance.

FIRST ELEVATOR

The first grain elevator in western Canada was constructed in Niverville in 1878. The cylindrical form was not used again until the 1980s, when concrete elevators were built to replace the traditional wooden ones.

Stonewall Lime Kilns

Photo courtesy of Earl Simmons

THESE DRAMATIC, MYSTERIOUS STRUCTURES look like something from the ancient past. But they're not ritualistic monuments, or chimneys venting some underground civilization. Their form, and their purpose are more mundane, but interesting nevertheless, important reminders of the character of early Manitoba industry.

The deposits of limestone around Stonewall and Garson have been the source of continuous industrial activity for more than a century. Around the town of Stonewall the beds of Ordovician-era limestone were first exploited as a quarry site in the mid-nineteenth century, providing distinctive limestone blocks for building projects. Then in the late 1800s Stonewall also became a major site for the production of lime, a product used in the production of various building products, particularly for mortar and cement.

The production of lime requires the heating and the consequent disintegration of stone into powder. The first so-called pot kilns were built in the late 1880s by William Bros. and were long, low structures requiring workers to spread limestone rocks over the tops and then light extensive fires underneath. All subsequent kilns were the distinctive vertical shafts that proved to be much more efficient.

John Gunn, a major figure in the local stone industry, built his kiln in 1900. The last were constructed in 1917. In total there were five kilns operating at Stonewall during the industry's heyday; the last one closed in 1968. Today several of the Stonewall quarries are still productive, and the quarries at Garson, where Manitoba's famous tyndall stone is extracted, provide beautiful stone for building projects all over the world.

While the rough technology required for the production of lime has been silent for more than 30 years, there are still plenty of people in Manitoba who recall the nature of the operations. Many claim that the thing they remember best is the sweet smell of burning wood from the fires that seemed to rage all day long.

The kilns at Stonewall were about 13 to 17 metres high, built of large blocks of limestone and lined with firebrick. Huge furnaces at the bottom of the structure were fuelled with wood in the early years and later with coal. Limestone chunks were carried to the top of the kiln via a ramp, and dumped into the top. A screen of iron rods kept the rock in place while heat reduced it to lime. Every three hours or so about 25 wheelbarrows of the stuff was drawn from the bottom and dumped into a box car. The whole process took about 36 hours, with each kiln producing about 15 tonnes per day.

QUICKLIME

- *The full name for lime is quicklime, defined as a white,*
- *caustic alkaline substance, whose chemical composition is*
- *calcium oxide, obtained by heating limestone and used for*
- *making mortar or as a fertilizer.*

McKenzie Seeds Building

REINFORCED CONCRETE IS PROBABLY NOT a subject that rates high on most people's list of great inventions. For those involved with the construction of many of Manitoba's buildings, however, it was a much-needed blessing when it was introduced in the early 20th century. Its discovery opened the door to various new structural possibilities. Most importantly it was imperative for the construction of massive multi-storied warehouses, and subsequently for other large scale building, whatever their purpose.

Before the inception of reinforced concrete the most common structural method employed for warehouses, where the weight of stored materials was immense, was to use heavy timbers connected in a framework of posts and beams. This technique provided adequate support, although it bore the potential to cause shifts and sags due to the wood's porous nature. There was also the additional concern about its lack of resistance to fire and heat. Concrete, embedded and strengthened with substantial steel reinforcing bars, offered a new and improved solution. It was stronger, less elastic, fireproof, and notably more enduring.

One of Manitoba's first reinforced concrete buildings was erected in Brandon. The McKenzie Seed Company Building was completed in 1910, and for 63 years was, at seven storeys in height, was the tallest building in the Wheat City. Today, only the eleven-storey Scotia Towers structure rises above it.

By 1905 the need for a building of this size was all too clear for the owners of McKenzie Seeds. Established in 1897 by Albert McKenzie (1870-1964), the operation was a booming enterprise, providing packaged garden seeds and related products to outlets all over Canada. By 1910 the operation was financially lucrative and growing, and three years later, in 1913, it was the largest seed company in western Canada. It was decided that a new facility capable of handling all the work, and the burgeoning orders, was required.

Brandon architect Thomas Sinclair produced a completely up-to-date building for Albert McKenzie. It was of the highest quality, reflective of its cost of $100,000. The interior public spaces employed plenty of costly marble. The building's handsome façade was sheathed with red brick, far more expensive than yellow brick commonly used at the time. And corners were highlighted with exquisite details of limestone. Underpinning this elegant outer architectural expression was the newly found reinforced concrete technology. Using what was called the "Turner-Mushroom" technique, large concrete columns were widened, or mushroomed, at the top to provide additional support to upper floors, each of which was also built with reinforced concrete.

While reinforced concrete technology may have been in its infancy when McKenzie Seeds was erected, it has stood the test of time, and the McKenzie Seeds Building is now an important and abiding Brandon landmark.

It's the 27-metre tower and elevators, added in 1918, that make the McKenzie Seeds Building a Brandon landmark, visible for several kilometres. At street level, the main building, seen in the inset, is also a notable feature in the city's architectural landscape.

Workers in 1958 inspect packets of the famous McKenzie Seeds Company product.

J.H. Ashdown Warehouse

The J.H. Ashdown Warehouse was but one exhibit of Ashdown's hardware empire. The warehouse supplied goods for his retail outlet on Main Street in Winnipeg, as well as to smaller facilities in Calgary, Edmonton, Saskatoon and Regina. Still nostalgically emblazoned on its south side with the imprint *The J.H. Ashdown Hardware Company Limited,* the warehouse has been converted to large, airy cube-style condominiums. Its dappled yellow brick and mighty square timber structure has been incorporated into the interior design of many of the fashionable apartments.

THE J.H. ASHDOWN WAREHOUSE, built in 1895, represented a new and increasingly popular warehouse design. Where earlier buildings were characterized by delightful and whimsical design, the architect for the Ashdown building S. Frank Peters was inspired by a more austere aesthetic first developed in the eastern United States.

In response to questions about the J.H. Ashdown Warehouse design Peters objected to describing it with a "high sounding name," but did say it was "in the modern commercial style." He was referring generally to a style of buildings constructed during the late 1880s in Chicago, and specifically to the works of the presiding genius of the new aesthetic Henry Hobson Richardson. Richardson's influence was so renowned and revered that it came to be applied to the style known as Richardsonian Romanesque.

Richardson's impressive buildings were noted for their exterior muscularity and unadorned honesty, which seamlessly reflected the contents of the Ashdown Warehouse: ploughs, nails, twine, wire, and shovels. All of the things needed by pioneers headed towards the prairies to stake out and build their homesteads.

During the 1890s and well into the 20th century Winnipeg's warehouse area, now known as the Exchange District, was a textbook collection of the Richardsonian Romanesque style. That many of these buildings still stand in the Exchange District is proof of their wholeness and solidity and the District has the distinctive designation of being a National Historic Site.

Like many other warehouses in Winnipeg, the Ashdown building was the subject of additions over the years, a response to Winnipeg's continued growth as the West's major wholesale centre. A flood of incoming settlers was unabated and the success of the wheat economy continued to drive the growth of Ashdown's enterprises. In 1899 he commissioned architect J.H.G. Russell to design a building, which he rented to the wholesale grocery firm Codville and Company, to the west of the original four-storey section. With a few smaller additions and subsequent extension of the whole complex by another two floors, Ashdown created one of the largest buildings in the area.

JAMES H. ASHDOWN (1844-1924)

Called Winnipeg's Merchant Prince and referred to as "the essence of the commercial spirit of the Western Canadian metropolis," James Ashdown was a large figure in Winnipeg's history. Born in London, England he immigrated with his family to Upper Canada in 1852, and made his way to the Red River Settlement in 1868. He opened his first store in 1869 and, as the Settlement grew, so did his business and his fortune. By 1910 Ashdown was a millionaire. He had spent time in Chicago before arriving in Manitoba, and appears to have been greatly influenced by his time there, determined to remake his adopted city in the former's image. He was active politically, supporting the anti-Riel forces during the Red River Rebellion and in 1874 headed the citizen's committee that secured incorporation for the City of Winnipeg. He served as an alderman and mayor in 1907 and 1908. He was also a founding member of the Board of Trade and served as its president in 1887. Throughout this time Ashdown built his hardware business into a manufacturing, wholesale and retail enterprise that dominated the hardware market in Western Canada for over sixty years, finally closing in 1970.

Leary's Brick Factory

THERE ARE THOUSANDS OF BRICK BUILDINGS in Manitoba from the late 19th and early 20th centuries that stand together as an important and sturdy legacy of the past. Only when one starts thinking of them as a group, however, does the question of the origins of the bricks themselves becomes a subject of interest.

In fact, most of those buildings were constructed using brick manufactured right in Manitoba. From about 1890 until just after World War I, dozens of brick factories operated in Manitoba, producing the millions and millions of bricks required as the province shifted from its pioneer stage to a mature society. The brick-making industry was so successful that some operations not only provided for local needs, but did a brisk business in exports, especially to the growing communities in the then-Northwest Territories and Regina in particular.

Some of these operations were small, others of considerable size, but they all shared one historically notable feature: few of them lasted more than ten years.

Brick factories typically arrived on the scene in the 1890s and early 1900s, nearly all of them located in the south-central and southwest of the province, where clay deposits were common and accessible. Enterprising people devoted considerable sums to building their operations. However, by the time the local building stock was remade in brick, or when the deposits of clay had been exhausted, most of the factories closed down. But not before creating a whole new province, architecturally, with buildings of yellow, red and even white brick.

Given the breadth of the industry, and the sturdiness of the structures required, it's surprising that only one complex has survived the years, a gem tucked in a valley in the Pembina Hills near St. Lupicin. And while the elemental forms of the old Leary's brick factory are starting to show their age, they are still powerful reminders of a once-vibrant industry.

George Leary's brick factory, about 50 kilometres west of Carman near St. Lupicin, is the last of a breed. Built in 1905, the powerful sculptural qualities of the remaining buildings—the dome of the kiln, the smoke stack and the steeply-pitched roof of the brick shed—are now poignant reminders of what was once a vibrant part of the province's economy.

HOW TO MAKE A BRICK

The raw material for Mr. Leary's brick factory—loose shale—was located in an opening in the nearby Pembina Hills. The shale was brought to the site where it was put through a crusher and ground to a fine grain. Mixed with water to make a stiff paste, the clay was then formed into bricks. The "green," or partially dried bricks were placed in the kiln, which could hold up to 80,000 bricks, and wood fires were burned, for up to 16 days. The first fires produced a low heat to remove moisture and carbon. Subsequent fires brought the kiln temperature to about 1200° C, the heat needed to fuse the clay. Once burned, the kiln was sealed and allowed to cool slowly for about two weeks.

Like most of the province's brick factories the substantial operation just outside of La Riviere operated for a brief time, just five years, from 1902 until 1907 and left few reminders of its once-major presence.

Railway Stables (The Forks)

Before the area behind Union Station was transformed into The Forks, it was known as the East Yards and was the site of major railway activity. In this old photograph the Canadian Northern Stable is visible on the right-hand side, set in a nest of railway tracks.

AT THE SAME TIME THAT RAILWAY COMPANIES were transforming the West in the late 19th and early 20th centuries, using the most up-to-date technologies like steam power and steel, they were also looking to the past for an important aspect of their business. For while it's true that the railways were creating a whole new way to travel and move goods, it was still horse-power that drove a great deal of the transportation industry.

When two of the major transcontinental rail services—Canadian Northern and Grand Trunk Pacific—combined forces in 1909 to build a major transportation centre in Winnipeg, at the foot of Broadway, the plan was for a complete transport hub. In addition to the impressive Union Station (page 82) and the luxurious Hotel Fort Garry (page 106), a whole set of utilitarian buildings placed behind, along the Red River, provided all sorts of service functions: a power plant, engine repair shops, turntable, warehouses, stables.

The two stables, one built in 1909 for the Canadian Northern Cartage Company, the other in 1910 for Grand Trunk Pacific, together accommodated about 220 horses and the wagons and carts needed in the operation. That fleet whisked goods arriving by train to various business interests throughout the city. For the next 25 years, until they were converted into garages, the buildings clattered with the sounds of hooves and the creak of wheels. For the interested observer, the area offered a fascinating dichotomy, with the mighty train locomotives roaring into Union Station to the west, while below the ancient traditions of horse and wagon went about their slow, stately ways.

The same architectural firm that created the elegant Union Station, Warren and Wetmore of New York City, was also commissioned to design the stable buildings. It couldn't have been particularly demanding work, but the firm still attempted to give these utilitarian buildings some architectural character. Distinctive archway entrances at either end of each building not only translated into broad interior arcades, they also provided the only notable architectural feature.

A SITE REBORN

During the late 1980s, the so-called Canadian National East Yards, and its valuable waterfront property, was redeveloped as The Forks, Winnipeg's premiere gathering spot. Respecting the site's railway history, the development re-used most of the historic buildings. The old horse stables of the Canadian Northern and Grand Trunk Pacific railways were gutted inside, cleaned up, and reworked with a new gallery link and a dramatic observation tower. As it turned out, the very character of the buildings—utilitarian, with simple forms, unadorned brick walls and large and numerous window openings—became the perfect foil as the architects created a whole new building.

HORSE POWER

Until well into the 1920s, wagons drawn by horses and oxen were common sights on Winnipeg streets. Besides the railway's cartage operations, the major department stores, dairies and ice manufacturers all operated significant horse-drawn fleets.

Lost Treasures — Industrial Sites

At the time when they would have been demolished, it is unlikely that many would have mourned the passing of most of historic Manitoba industrial sites. They were dirty. They were smelly. And of course, because they were often strictly utilitarian buildings, they were thought to have few redeeming architectural qualities.

Things look different now. Those buildings have become respected and valued pieces of our heritage. They were where our forebears worked, and because of that they resonate with proud labour. Some survive, but many, like the few shown here, have been lost.

VIEW NEAR FORT GARRY.

Logan's Windmill. Lord Selkirk's first crop of settlers, arriving at Red River in 1812, had many other things on their minds besides agriculture; foremost: survival. However, by the 1820s, some success had been gained with cereal grains and a rudimentary farming economy was in place. One of the most important elements in the infrastructure was the mill, powered by wind or water (with wind the more common vehicle), by which settlers could have their grain ground into flour. Between 1830 and 1870, more than 100 windmills and 20 water mills were built throughout the Settlement.

Robert Logan's windmill was a well known Red River landmark, built in 1825 and running for more than 40 years, a familiar site on what is now Point Douglas. In this rendering, an unknown artist has captured in considerable detail the character and operation of the windmill. It's a cap mill, a technical distinction describing those operations whose sails could be turned into the wind by the movement of a rotating section at the top. It's also small, a rudimentary structure, and the sails (in this case without their canvas coverings, needed to actually operate the mill) are small, suggesting the limited capacity of the operation.

Gunn's Water Mill. The fortuitous recording of Bruce Gunn's detailed and entertaining recollections in the local history book, *East Side of the Red* (1984) allow for this rendering of the water mill constructed by his father in the early 1850s. As Bruce Gunn recalled, "On his homestead, a creek [wound] sleepily in and out through beautiful groves of oak and elm [and occasionally went] on periodic rampages. Here was water power [and] there was wheat to be ground. What more logical, in the premises, than a watermill? When necessary to grind at night, some sort of fish-oil lamps, suspended at convenient points, were used. Nearly all the machinery housed in the structure was, a year or so prior growing in the forest or reposing peaceful in its native habitat. With the exception of a few small metal gear wheels, brought by Mississippi steamer and Red River cart from St. Louis and some brass bolting cloth from England, every wheel and spindle and every other working part was manufactured from local materials by local artisans."

Drewry's Brewery. One of the province's first breweries was established in Winnipeg in 1881 by Edward Drewry. The old brewing complex, on the Red River at Redwood Avenue, was a landmark for anyone who knew their beer, producing ales, porters, stouts and lagers. The original complex, seen here in the 1890s, was much-altered over the years, and was only recently demolished after being operated for many years by Carling-O'Keefe.

Vulcan Iron Works. Winnipeg's Point Douglas area, the site of early settlement in 1812 by the Selkirk Settlers, had by the late 19th century become a favoured site for industry. The location of the Canadian Pacific Railway's main line right through its middle attracted such concerns as warehouses, lumber yards, paint, drug, vinegar and pickle factories and manufacturers of bedding and carriages. One of the largest concerns was the Vulcan Iron Works. While a section of the original complex still stands, on the north side of Sutherland Street, most of it has been lost.

HOTEL FORT GARRY

METROPOLITAN THEATRE

GRANITE CURLING CLUB

DARLINGFORD WAR MEMORIAL

VIRDEN AUDITORIUM

ASSINIBOINE PARK PAVILION

LOST TREASURES

Chapter 8

8

RECREATIONAL

Hotel Fort Garry

THE HOTEL FORT GARRY IS ONE of Manitoba's most glamorous buildings.

The hotel has been the site of innumerable events of high drama, and has hosted guests of great distinction, like Prince Charles, Harry Belafonte, Nelson Eddy, Charles Laughton, Laurence Olivier, Liberace and Louis Armstrong. The hotel's sumptuous halls, spaces and rooms are justly famous for their high quality and expensive finishes.

It has been a favourite destination and a landmark since its construction in 1912-13, its architectural quality the source of local pride. But maybe the enduring fondness also rests at a subconscious level, where the building's design and style speaks to certain qualities of its citizens. Actually, that was the intent of its architects, and especially of certain authorities in Ottawa who were determined at this time to create a distinctly "Canadian" style of architecture.

This kind of nationalist thinking began in the United States, around the time of the American Centennial of 1876, where a vigorous debate sought to determine an "American" style. The famous architectural firm McKim, Mead and White (whose Bank of Montreal in Winnipeg is discussed on page 86) were at the vanguard of this movement, seeking inspiration from their own past, particularly American Colonial architecture of the 1700s, both from examples created by architects, but also from vernacular traditions.

In Canada a similar debate focused on two options as most expressive of a national style. Many architects and writers promoted what was called the High Gothic Revival (like the Parliament Buildings in Ottawa). Others felt the British connections to this version of the Gothic Revival excluded the heritage of Quebec, and promoted medieval French châteaux as more inclusive (the Château Laurier Hotel in Ottawa was the model for these proponents). The Château style was seen as combining the country's French and British roots, and was also popular because of its association with railways, the country's great connector.

By 1927 the choice of the Château style was federal policy, as evinced by a report to the Department of Public Works, in which past and present chief architects recommended that "new government building should be Gothic in character and suggest [the] Norman French Gothic Type."

Interesting, certainly. The thought that this hotel expresses some part of our being Canadian.

This dramatic photograph, from around 1914, shows the new hotel to good effect, and also reveals the relationship between it and the reason for its creation, the Winnipeg terminus for the Grand Trunk Pacific Railway (GTP), seen to its left, at the foot of Broadway, Union Station. The GTP was the third major rail company to undertake a transcontinental Canadian rail service, along with the Canadian Pacific Railway and Canadian Northern (which partnered with the GTP in the construction of the station). By 1920 Grand Trunk was in receivership and in 1923 was amalgamated with Canadian Northern to create Canadian National.

Perched like mountaineers on a steep summit, workers put the finishing touches on the copper sheathing atop the Hotel Fort Garry.

Like many grand hotels, the Fort Garry was home to scores of support staff, like these waiters posing in January of 1921.

A LITANY OF LUXURY

As this random sampling of observant quotes from a contemporary review of the new hotel suggests, this was indeed a sumptuous feast for the senses (from *Construction Magazine,* June 1914).

> Everywhere are scattered flower vases and boxes modeled in cream terra-cotta after the best examples of Italian work; oak divans and chairs upholstered in Spanish leather or tapestry finished with brass studs, depicting the age of Louis XIV.
>
> The marble floor [is] of Napoleon gray [marble] inlaid with Belgian block [and] is given the restfulness of the other fittings by means of two large heavy hand-tufted Donegal rugs.
>
> In the rotunda facing the main office stands a master clock artistically carved in solid oak. It is fitted with an electric device for synchronizing it with the time at the Government observatory; the connection being made by means of direct wire communication.
>
> The windows here [in the mezzanine] as throughout the ground floor, consist of metal frames and the best quality of British polished plate glass.
>
> The walls [of the ladies' drawing room] are hung in silk amber panels, terminating in an acanthus leaf moulding.
>
> To the right of the rotunda is the stairway of Hauteville marble, possessing a heavy iron bronze balustrade extremely rich in design.
>
> The soffit of the beams [in the main dining room] are also ornnamented in low relief with models of a pine cone, laurel, tulip and other features typical of Canadian life.

THE CHÂTEAU STYLE

Large, luxurious hotels were built by competing railway companies across Canada as magnets for their clientele. The trend began in 1892 with the start of construction, by the CPR, of the Château Frontenac Hotel in Quebec City, and

gained momentum in 1912 with the completion by the GTP of the Château Laurier Hotel in Ottawa. The Grand Trunk Pacific had commissioned Montreal architects Ross and MacFarlane for the Laurier, and stayed with them for their new venture in Winnipeg, originally to be called the Selkirk Hotel. The preferred style for these memorable buildings was the Château style, a romantic, picturesque style based on French Gothic castles of Normandy. Those qualities also found their way inside where for example this ornate railing detail was used.

Metropolitan Theatre

THE ALLEN THEATRE, later the Metropolitan, opened in Winnipeg in 1920 in the same year that the great silent movie director D.W. Griffith made *Way Down East*. That famous film, with its wild scenes in the snow and the climactic scene on a dangerous ice floe, must have resonated with audiences in Winnipeg. As was reviewed in the *New York Times* in September of that year, "Anna Moore, the wronged heroine of *Way Down East*, was turned out into the snowstorm again last evening, but it was such a blizzard as she had never been turned out into in all the days since Lottie Blair Parker first told her woes nearly 25 years ago [the story from which the film was adapted]. For this was the screen version of that prime old New England romance, and the audience that sat in rapture at the Forty-fourth Street theatre to watch its first unfolding here realized finally why it was D.W. Griffith has selected it for a picture. It was not for its fame. Nor for its heroine. Not for the wrong done her. It was for the snowstorm. True, here and there comes a suggestion of papier-mâché danger, of studio ice, of dummy figures and all that, but for the most part it is uncommonly well done, and the effect is breathtaking. Any audience would have cheered it, and all audiences will." Winnipeggers could relate to snowstorms.

Moving pictures, that great invention of the turn of the century, were at this time not a novelty in Winnipeg. For at least a decade before the Allen was built, audiences sat enraptured in small venues—arcades, vaudeville houses, even the backs of stores—watching the quirky magic of silent films. Instant classics like the nine-minute *The Great Train Robbery* from 1903 or *The Perils of Pauline* from 1914; and the not-so-classic, *Broncho Billy and the Baby* of 1908, or *The Angel of Dawson's Claim* from 1910.

What was new was the creation of the palaces in which to enjoy a night on the town. Sumptuous, glamorous and exotic—everything Hollywood offered—were the bywords. And the arrival of the Allen Brothers chain, from Ontario, and the construction of their theatre, ushered in an era where the movie and the movie-house dominated the weekend.

The Metropolitan Theatre, built in 1919 and opened in 1920, was designed in Detroit by C.H. Crane. The architect employed a style popularized in the United States by Charles Lamb, at the time the leading designer of opera houses and the newly emerging movie theatre. Lamb and his successors found a perfect architectural expression for these kinds of buildings in what was called the Adamesque Georgian style. At the Metropolitan, Crane used the elegant possibilities of that style to create a sumptuous building across from the Eaton's Store. The highlights of the carefully crafted façade were seven delicately detailed windows. Framed by fluted pilasters, each window was protected by a wrought iron faux balcony, and capped with terra cotta ornamentation.

ACADEMY THEATRE

In 1931 Allied Amusements upped the ante for local theatre designs with this fantastic Moorish palace by Winnipeg architect Max Blankstein. Still standing in all its glory, it is now a bowling lane.

This view of the interior, which could hold about 2,500 people, shows, at the front of the stage, the orchestra pit, in which musicians accompanied the silent action on screen.

LILLIAN GISH

The star of Way Down East, *one of the big box office smashes of 1920, was one of the great stars of the Silent Era. A favourite of the directorial master of the age, D.W. Griffith, she epitomized for him exquisite fragility and ethereal beauty. She starred in dozens of his films, including* Birth of a Nation *(1915) and* Intolerance *(1916).*

For these great pioneers of the movie industry, silent films were more than entertainment. As Griffith told Gish, "You are working in the universal language that was predicted in the Bible, which was to make all men brothers because they would understand each other. This could end wars and bring about the millennium."

Granite Curling Club

ONE OF THE KEY TECHNICAL REQUIREMENTS of a curling club predicated why the Granite Curling Club was located on the banks of the Assiniboine River. It wasn't the view, or the prestigious location. It had to do with ice. Or at least, water. Lots of water. For years, it was necessary to draw huge amounts of water from the river to create the nine sheets of ice at The Granite.

At the time it was built in 1913 this proximity to the river was a key consideration as the members of the club debated where to move their club, after deciding in 1911 that their Hargrave and Ellice building was too small. The Granite was the city's first curling club, established in 1881, and has been home to several provincial, national and world champions. It established the first indoor rink in Winnipeg in 1892 and for years was one of only three rinks that served the city.

With their new building the members of The Granite were determined to make a statement. The architects, James Chisholm and his son C.C., were considered two of the best in the city; C.C. was also an avid curler and President of the Manitoba Curling Association in 1921-22. When all was said and done, the new building cost a-then astronomical $140,000. It was nearly double the cost of the facility erected by the Thistle Club in 1912, and about ten times the cost of the Fort Rouge Curling Club that went up in 1919.

The Granite was a palace for the sport. And though many of the members were amongst the city's well-to-do, The Granite soon found itself over-extended, unable to pay the mortgage and the taxes. In 1916 the Government of Manitoba took over the club and rented it back to the club for the next 30 years.

The architects of the Granite Curling Club, James Chisholm and his son C.C., created a building that was deemed by its membership to be an appropriate architecture for expressing the attributes of the game. The use of English Tudor half-timbering connected it to curling's national roots: England, via Scotland. And the crenellated military towers at each corner were intended to remind people of the manly character of the game. For curling was deemed by many in the city as the perfect Manitoba sport, to be played by men of character in the dead of winter as a test of vigour, endurance, determination, concentration, planning and cooperation.

CURLING, CIRCA 1908

The first women's curling club in Manitoba was formed in 1908, and was associated with The Granite. For women, the sport was considered an acceptable activity for the feminine qualities of grace, elegance and modesty.

Darlingford War Memorial

The Darlingford War Memorial was designed by Arthur Stoughton, founder of the School of Architecture at the University of Manitoba, and its first professor and head from 1913-29. Its exterior is powerful in spite of its small size, with a steep roof and rich patterns created by the brickwork. Inside, the stark white walls and the absence of seating demand silence and respect. Arrayed against the walls are plaques, weapons and other war memorabilia.

PSYCHIC WOUNDS would have been fresh when the Darlingford War Memorial was dedicated on July 5, 1921. It had been almost three years since the end of the Great War, but the unbelievable losses—7,760 from Manitoba alone—ruined so many lives that it seemed impossible that anyone would ever regain a sense of joy and hope. But on that hot, sunny, summer day, it seemed like the wounds suffered by the people of Darlingford might actually have begun to repair.

The dedication service for the memorial was presided over by its main proponent Ferris Bolton, the Member of Parliament for Lisgar. The day started at the local CPR station, where the whole village of Darlingford gathered to greet two visiting dignitaries from Winnipeg, Lieutenant-Governor Sir James Aikins and Major-General Huntley Ketchen. From the station, the proceedings continued with a parade led by local school children, followed by the visiting Morden Brass Band and a military guard. At the memorial, emotional speeches were made, wreathes were laid and a scripture lesson was read. At the conclusion of the ceremony the school children formed themselves into the shape of a cross and everyone joined in singing *Nearer My God to Thee* and the National Anthem. The day ended with a banquet, baseball tournament and a moving picture show in the local skating rink.

So simple, heartfelt and poignant. One could almost, for a moment, forget the unimaginably sorrowful purpose of the memorial and of Ferris Bolton's great loss.

Ferris Bolton (1853-1937) was a pioneer in the Darlingford area, by 1910 a successful farmer, and with his wife Elizabeth, the proud father of four boys and a girl. His life was good. When war was declared in August of 1914, however, three of the Bolton boys were quick to enlist. The beloved boys never returned. Bert, aged 22, was killed at Vimy Ridge. Harry was struck down at Lens, at the age of 20. Elmer, only 18, was killed at Hill 70, a battle site north of Lens. The loss of their three sons, all in 1917, as well as the 15 other local boys, so touched Bolton that he donated the land on which to erect a war memorial in their honour.

His idea was unique. Instead of the statue, or municipal hospital, or community hall suggested by others, Bolton's idea called for the creation of a memorial building set in a miniature park, treed, with flower beds and walks. His idea prevailed.

Eighty years later, the wisdom of that choice is profound. On a hot August day, when the wheat fields that surround the village are turning to gold, this green oasis, and the delicate little building at its heart, is both a balm and a reminder of what could have been but never was.

A photograph from the 1921 dedication ceremony for the Darlingford War Memorial.

Virden Opera House

IN 1911 THE TOWN OF VIRDEN decided that its burgeoning population, and its status as one of the province's major communities, demanded a new civic centre. The old one consisted of a set of offices that were part of the fire hall constructed in 1895. The town proposed to build a new structure beside the fire hall. The highlight of the enterprise, however, was not the new town office. It was the opera house that was to be included.

Today it seems like a peculiar combination of functions—fire hall, town hall and opera house—but for several communities building their town halls around the turn of the century, it was often assumed that a necessary component of the building had to be an opera house, or at least an auditorium. City halls in Winnipeg and Brandon had one, as did smaller facilities in places like Manitou and Neepawa. Such amenities were considered important civic responsibilities, providing citizens with the opportunity to enjoy theatrical and vaudeville productions, and to attend political rallies.

The term "opera house" overstates the function. In turn-of-the-century Manitoba the opera was usually more a vaudeville show, although travelling theatrical troupes were also frequent visitors. The local opera house was often housed in modest circumstances, usually above a store or office. By 1910 the term "opera house," and the live performances it showcased, were becoming obsolete, displaced in many communities by the theatre, a new kind of facility in which photo plays, or silent films, were displayed.

In Virden, the new civic building was completed and in February of 1912 the first play, *The Misogynist*, was staged by a local amateur company. The debut of a professional troupe was by the Allen Players who performed Tolstoy's *Resurrection*. The "Aud" became home to the Virden Dramatic and Operatic Society and the Virden Orchestra, and soon became the social and entertainment centre for the performing arts in western Manitoba.

Designed by W.A. Elliott of Brandon, the new building provided access from the street into the new Town Office, and then at the back into the Auditorium. The "Aud" was closed in 1980, and the adjacent fire hall was demolished in 1981. Determined to save this historic reminder of the town's proud theatrical past, the community worked in 1982-83 to save the "Aud," and to rebuild a section reminiscent of the fire hall.

INTERIOR GRANDEUR

Inside, the Auditorium was Virden's prize, capable of seating fully a third of the town's population. The Great Eastern Scene Painting Company of Toronto did the scenic painting at a cost of $947. Theatre seats were purchased from Andrew and Co., of Chicago, at between $2.13 and $2.44 each.

The Virden Dramatic and Operatic Society decked out for their 1915 production of *The Mikado*.

The Pavilion in Assiniboine Park replaced a building that burned in 1929. The new building, designed by Winnipeg architects Northwood and Chivers, opened on May 29, 1930.

Assiniboine Park Pavilion

ONE OF MANITOBA'S BEST KNOWN BUILDINGS, the Pavilion in Winnipeg's Assiniboine Park, has only recently seen its function change to more accurately reflect its impressive architectural quality. For years this beautiful and beloved building, an outstanding example of English Tudor half-timbering, with its delicate pergola and lily pond at the back, was actually a glorified hot dog stand.

In 1997 the Pavilion became the focus for a major redevelopment. The upper floors were reworked as an art gallery displaying works of art by three of Manitoba's most distinguished artists, Ivan Eyre, Clarence Tillenius and Walter J. Phillips. And on the ground floor—the former site of hot dogs and french fries and soft drinks—an elegant restaurant now looks out onto the leafy pergola behind.

DON'T LOOK TWICE

It was the floor plan of John D. Atchison's first Assiniboine Park Pavilion, built in 1908 and destroyed by fire in 1929, that guided architects Northwood and Chivers in their design for the new building. But they also reiterated the basic form and tower that Atchison had created.

Lost Treasures — Recreational Buildings

Hotels, those once-grand symbols of Victorian luxury and exuberant architectural style are sadly missed. But there have been other losses too, and as the buildings showcased here suggest, it is a vacancy in Manitoba's architectural heritage that cannot be repaired.

Dance Hall, Grand Beach, 1915. The old dance hall on the east shore of Lake Winnipeg was razed in a fire in 1950.

Manitoba Hotel, Winnipeg, 1891. The first grand hotel in Winnipeg, constructed by the Grand Trunk Pacific Railway, the Manitoba was destroyed by fire in 1899. It was located on Main Street, near Water Avenue. Shortly after its demise the Industrial Bureau Exposition Building (right) was constructed on its former location.

Industrial Bureau Exposition Building, Winnipeg, 1912, John D. Atchison. This once-dramatic presence at the corner of Main Street and Water Avenue was removed to make way for the Federal Building of 1935, which is still standing today.

Prince Edward Hotel, Brandon, 1912, Pratt and Ross. This luxurious Canadian Northern Railway hotel, complete with a railway terminal at the back, was a beloved Brandon landmark that was demolished in 1980.

Main Building, Winnipeg Industrial Exhibition, 1891, Charles Burgess. Lost long ago.

Royal Alexandra Hotel, Winnipeg, 1904-06. One of the city's finest hotels was deemed redundant by the Canadian Pacific Railway and demolished in 1971.

Chapter 9

9

MODERN BUILDINGS

Stonewall Post Office

THE STONEWALL POST OFFICE, constructed in 1914-15, was one of Manitoba's first "modern" buildings and was influenced by the sophisticated design attitudes of the great American architect Frank Lloyd Wright. Instead of being cast in one of the traditional historical styles that marked nearly all public buildings at the time, particularly Gothic or Classical, the Stonewall Post Office was fashioned in the new Prairie Style, a design philosophy that was conceived by Wright around the turn of the century.

But, the Stonewall Post Office was not only influenced by Wright; it can actually claim a small, yet impressive connection to the world-renowned architect. Francis Conroy Sullivan, its designer, was an Ottawa architect who was an acolyte of Wright who worked off and on for nearly 20 years in the great man's studios, and on several of his most important buildings.

Sullivan (1882-1929) began his career as a draftsman and architect in the Chief Architect's Office of the Department of Public Works in Ottawa. In 1911 he resigned his post, seeking greater challenges, and moved his young family to Chicago where he worked in Wright's Oak Park office on the design for the Pembroke Ontario Public Library.

By 1913 Sullivan was back in Ottawa, and back in the Public Works department where he used his newfound observations of Wright's creations to design the Stonewall Post Office. It must have caused a stir in his office, where the prevailing stylistic choice was Classical Revival, a tried-and-true style that imbued buildings with a sense of grandeur and delight.

After 1916 Sullivan's career declined and he moved to Taliesin, Wisconsin, Wright's new design Mecca, where he worked on the drawings for the Imperial Hotel in Tokyo. But there was something self-destructive about Sullivan's behaviour—he has been described as eccentric, difficult, temperamental—so while his early career showed great promise, for the next ten years he eked out a living doing small jobs in other architects' offices. When his wife finally divorced him, in 1927, he seems to at once have been conversely shattered yet eased. He spent the last few years of his life at Taliesen West, outside Phoenix, Arizona, in the company of the designers he revered and, of course, alongside his hero Frank Lloyd Wright.

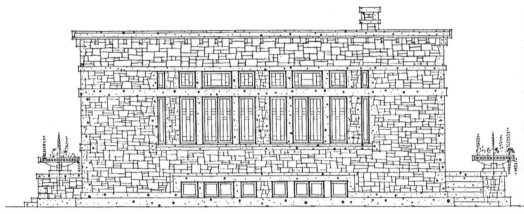

ELEVATION ON JACKSON AVE.

FRANK LLOYD WRIGHT IN MANITOBA

Architect Francis Sullivan undoubtedly pored over Frank Lloyd Wright's 1908 essays "In the Cause of Architecture," wherein Sullivan set forth his architectural tenets, and found the inspiration that would lead to his design for the Stonewall Post Office. In this seminal work Wright enunciated how a building (and for Wright "a building" usually meant a house) should possess simplicity and repose, qualities that should be articulated in various ways. The floor plan should be simplified so as to contain a minimal number of rooms; openings should occur as integral features of the structure and form; ornament should be avoided; fixtures and furniture should be designed as constituent parts of the house; the building should appear to grow easily from its site, with gently sloping (even flat) roofs, low proportions, quiet sky lines, suppressed chimneys and sheltering overhangs, low terraces and outreaching walls sequestering quiet gardens; colours should harmonize with those of nature, the soft warm optimistic tones of earth and autumn leaves in preference to the pessimistic blues, purples or cold greens and grays of the ribbon counter; and finally, materials should reveal their natural colours and textures.

Sullivan's design for the Stonewall Post Office is an embodiment of these tenets, with one interesting departure from Wright's typical approach. Where Wright relied almost exclusively on brick for the walls of most of his houses in this period, the plenitude of limestone at Stonewall likely drew Sullivan to experiment with the effects of that material, further enhancing the indigenous and natural integration of the building's façades with the gold of the nearby prairie crops. The old post office was designated as a Provincial Heritage Site in 1989 and is now an art gallery and café.

Treesbank Bridge

THERE IS A COLLECTION OF CONCRETE BRIDGES in southwestern Manitoba that recalls the roots of Manitoba's inventive civil engineering profession. These bridges, most of which cross the Assiniboine and Souris rivers are, in a word, beautiful.

During the 1920s and 1930s the provincial government embarked on an ambitious programme that saw scores of bridges erected in rural areas. These structures were part of an important effort to improve the rural roads system and consequently to foster greater economic development across the province. Under the direction of M.A. Lyons, Chief Engineer for the Good Roads Branch of the Provincial Department of Public Works, and first President of the Association of Professional Engineers of Manitoba, a team of talented and determined young people undertook the design and construction of what has become an amazing legacy of bridge architecture.

Often consisting of reinforced concrete, poured into forms, many of these bridges were exquisite examples of design, marrying fine engineering with a delightful aesthetic sensibility. There were three basic types: a simple post-and-beam configuration; monolithic barrel-vaulted structures; and the most impressive, elegant designs with Bowstring, Through or Parabolic arches. Examining the whole collection suggests the high levels of innovation that attended the bridge-designing office. Each bridge was different, and the variety of designs implies a team that was pushed to explore the possibilities of poured concrete and the use of the arch.

The bridge near Treesbank is one of the finest of the lot, featuring a distinctive set of graceful Bowstring arches curving sensuously above two elegant piers. The bridge, which is still used more than eighty years after its construction, is one of more than a dozen monuments that still stand as a testament to these imaginative bridge-builders.

DELIGHTFUL

The Arden Bridge and the Millwood Bridge, both constructed in 1920, are excellent examples of arched bridge construction in the province. The Arden Bridge is a Through arch, in which the weight of the span, and of the vehicles that pass over it, are transferred down to the sides of the banks of the Whitemud River. The Millwood Bridge, which crosses the Assiniboine River, is a fine example of a barrel vault design. The powerful, elemental shapes are reminiscent of the ancient bridges of Rome and Paris.

The double Bowstring arches and three spans of the bridge that crosses the Assiniboine River just north of Treesbank was built in 1921 and was designed by E.S. Kent, one of the young engineers of the Provincial Good Roads Branch.

Civic Auditorium

THE GREAT DEPRESSION OF THE 1930S caused hardship in nearly every part of the Prairie economy, with the most dramatic decline in the farming sector, which produced tremendous personal loss for families, but also resulted in the abandonment of farmsteads. Other sectors followed the decline as the Depression made its grim and determined way through the decade. Thousands of workers were laid off in the manufacturing and industrial sectors.

With increasing hardships afflicting more and more people it became clear that governments would have to take action. One of the more successful solutions was found in large public works projects, especially in the construction of major public buildings. These projects not only offered much-needed work to those involved in the industry—architects, carpenters, masons—but also to hundreds of other men and women whose unskilled labour was put to good use.

In Winnipeg the first major relief project, costing $1 million, and paid for by funds from federal, provincial and municipal coffers, was the Civic Auditorium, built in 1932. Three local architectural firms—Northwood and Chivers, Col. John Semmens; and Pratt and Ross—shared the commission. The project provided work to skilled tradespeople, but also for work gangs of unskilled men, who dug out the basement and foundation using only spades, and to draymen, who carried away the earth in horse-drawn wagons.

When it was finished, the Civic Auditorium (nick-named The Aud) was a source of great civic pride. In the city's unstinting efforts to regain economic prosperity, The Aud was billed in contemporary pamphlets as the city's Convention Centre, and as a jewel in the architectural firmament. The Aud proved a wise investment, providing nights of entertainment, levity, and distraction during a bleak and depressing decade.

ART DECO

The Civic Auditorium was one of Winnipeg's early examples of Art Deco design. While that style was still proudly decorative—the faceted wall surfaces and exquisitely carved stone details were based on jewelery design—it marked an important break with the historical styles that held sway throughout the nineteenth and early twentieth centuries.

A STYLE'S ORIGINS

The Art Deco style had its roots in jewellry design and was highly influenced by the faceted geometric shapes that were possible in the cutting of gems. This lamp, which lights another Art Deco building in Winnipeg, the Women's Tribute Building, is a fine example of this aesthetic.

This photograph—of the opening gala of the Civic Auditorium in November of 1932—suggests an important calculation in the building's design and architectural appointments—the interior was shaped like a school gymnasium, stripped down to its bare essentials. Nearly all of the finer embellishments were reserved for the exterior, where the public had a better chance, albeit a free chance, to behold them during cash-strapped times. In the mid -1970s the building was gutted to accommodate the Provincial Archives of Manitoba.

Winnipeg Clinic

TAKE A MINUTE TO EXAMINE this well-known Winnipeg landmark and you will quickly discover that it is really two buildings. Look upward and here's the fabulous, finned, space-age tower from the early 1960s, where cartoon character George Jetson would have felt right at home. Cast your eyes lower and you will see on the lower storeys of the west side another, older structure, a smallish Art Moderne gem from 1942.

Additions onto buildings—even vertical additions—are not unusual. Many warehouses in Winnipeg's Exchange District were designed with extra-strength foundations and thick brick walls to support additional floors when businesses needed to expand. What the designers of these warehouses didn't do was construct a whole new building on top of, or adjacent to, the original; they usually sought instead to create seamless, integrated extensions that blended perfectly with the original, mostly using the same materials, colours, details, window size and placement.

When you look at the original Winnipeg Clinic built in 1942 you can appreciate the challenges—and opportunities—the owners faced in their expansion efforts. Most of these came down to the limitations created by the original building. Firstly, that building's foundation had not been designed to accept further additions, so the possibility of adding vertically on top was out. Secondly, Art Moderne as a style had seen its day, and the doctors of the clinic must have wanted to embrace a new, more current interpretation of their time.

The most significant Art Moderne building in Manitoba, the Toronto-Dominion Bank of 1951-52, was demolished in the 1980s to make way for the TD Centre. Designed by Northwood and Chivers of Winnipeg and W. and W.S.R.L. Blackwood and Craig of Toronto, this important early-50s bank was a compromise between style and function. The typical sweeping curve and horizontal banding that define the Moderne style are present here, but bank officials likely could not completely disown the historical style that had helped enoble and advertise their bread-and-butter operations for nearly seven decades: Classical Revival. Here, the echoes of that vocabulary can be seen in the much-flattened pilasters on the main floor and the cornice at the roof ridge.

In 1947, just five years after the construction of the original Art Moderne building, with its dramatically curved façade and large bank of glass blocks, the E.R. Lount Construction Company was commissioned to design and erect a whole new building beside the original. By the early 1960s the clinic once again needed more space and this time the Lount Company opted for a five-storey addition to its Space Age fantasy, seen at the right.

Shaarey Zedek Synagogue

IN THE EARLY NINETEENTH CENTURY, European aesthetic theorists argued that to be outstanding a building needed to express its function through meaningful historic associations. This was thought to be especially true for religious buildings, with their profound expressions of faith and culture. The architects of Catholic and Protestant churches looked to medieval precedents, adapting Romanesque and Gothic designs to contemporary needs. Synagogue architects, however, found themselves at a loss. There was no clear and obvious architectural tradition to look back on, the result of centuries of forced migration and anti-semitic exclusion from the building trades. An attenuated version of the Romanesque style was attempted, but designers quickly turned to Oriental styles, particularly Egyptian and Moorish, seen more commonly in the Middle East. However, even these solutions did not meet theorists' strict standards, and synagogue designs of the nineteenth century were seen as generally too individualistic to attain the ubiquity that defined other faiths' houses of worship.

In Manitoba—Winnipeg and Brandon especially—small Jewish populations had built several modest synagogues since their arrival here beginning in the 1870s. These buildings were generally conceived as functional halls with fanciful façade treatments. European highbrows would not have been impressed, but the pretensions of the architectural and intellectual elite were not to last. The historicist approach to architecture began to wane in the early twentieth century and as all building types were shed of their need to obey conventions and traditions, the synagogue as a building type was ripe for exploration.

The construction in general, and the location in particular, in 1949 of Shaarey Zedek Synagogue marked a profound shift in design in many ways for Manitoba Jews. The building featured a highly sophisticated and sleek design, in a universally accepted style. It was produced by one of the city's most respected firms—Green, Blankstein and Russell. It was situated on a prime piece of property south of the Assiniboine River, and recessed into the slope of the Assiniboine riverbank, angled to feature prominently on the busiest corner of Wellington Crescent, still home to many of Winnipeg's wealthiest families and biggest mansions. The new building thus symbolized, on many levels, the pride and determination of the Jewish community in Winnipeg.

BETH JACOB SYNAGOGUE

The flamboyant façade of the demolished Beth Jacob Synagogue was one of Winnipeg's most ambitious and splendid synagogues of the early twentieth century featuring a playful mix of Oriental ornamentation.

The first Shaarey Zedek (which translates as "Gates of Righteousness") Synagogue was built in 1890 to designs by Charles Wheeler, one of the city's foremost architects. Sixty years later the new Shaarey Zedek Synagogue of 1949 was built to designs of one of the city's most acclaimed architectural firms of the day, Green, Blankstein, Russell, who were in the forefront of Manitoba's Modernist Movement. Their design for the synagogue was an impressive review of the tenets of Modernism. The building was a complex aggregation of cubic forms, deftly handled to define the several internal functions that were required. Window and door openings were like the overall form, highly varied but also clearly of a family—tall and thin.

NEW HALLS OF WORSHIP

Religious architecture in the twentieth century has been characterized by a dramatic and exciting exploration of the form and function of the building type. Architects have found inspiration in the many new styles advanced over the years. Increasingly they have looked to the sculptural opportunities suggested by a faith, and also to the vernacular traditions that often have been eschewed in the search for the sublime. The three churches highlighted here only suggest the dynamic range of designs that enlivened the architectural dialogue in the last half of the twentieth century in Manitoba.

ST. MICHAEL'S UKRAINIAN CATHOLIC CHURCH, TYNDALL

This church was an important commission for the Ukrainian-born architect Radoslav Zuk, who, after a stint at the University of Manitoba became a professor at McGill University's School of Architecture. The church has unfortunately been lost, a victim of highway widening in the 1990s. The building, completed in 1962, was an important break with tradition in the Ukrainian Catholic community. Zuk looked to the rich folk traditions of Ukrainian architecture in this building. At the Tyndall church, Zuk recalled architecture from the Boyko region of western Ukraine, where the traditional church was distinguished by three pyramidal roofs, the central one taller than the others. This appropriation is not literal, however and so the Boyko trinity was set atop the three towers that contained the stained glass windows. The walls were faced with Tyndallstone, the locally-quarried limestone that has made this little community a household word in Manitoba.

PRECIOUS BLOOD ROMAN CATHOLIC CHURCH, WINNIPEG

Architects Etienne Gaboury and Denis Lussier conceived this dramatically-shaped church as a conical spiral, to physically represent the Roman Catholic's journey to God. In this version, built in 1967-68, the spiral is not a clean, pure form. It is marked by a jagged, even rough quality, expressed especially in the natural cedar shingles that cover the undulating roof—emphasizing the struggles inherent in such a journey. The roofline also draws onlookers' eyes upward and around, further emphasizing the often circuitous and monumental nature of faith.

THUNDERBIRD HOUSE, WINNIPEG

Thought by Native peoples to be the guardian of mankind against the serpent of the underworld, the Thunderbird is a super eagle, capable of transforming itself into a man and able to create lightning by flashing its eyes. Thunderbird House, located in central Winnipeg, is Métis architect Douglas Cardinal's built manifestation of this creature. A ring of turquoise glass and natural timber posts define the ground level, while the powerful downspread wings of the mighty copper eagle provides shelter and inspiration.

Winnipeg Civic Centre

IN 1954 A GROUP OF ARCHITECTURE STUDENTS at the University of Manitoba, under the direction of Professor Herschel Elarth, produced an important article for the Journal of the Royal Architectural Institute of Canada. Entitled "Red River Skyline", it was on one hand a brief history and critique of Manitoba's architectural past, but it was also a call to arms, a manifesto for the Modern Movement in architecture. And in many ways it set the stage for scores of new buildings in Manitoba, including the Winnipeg Civic Centre of 1963-65.

The authors quickly established their thesis, which was a search in architecture for the honest, the basic, and the true. That is, in the tenets of Modern architecture as espoused by the great European masters of the 1920s: Le Corbusier, Walter Gropius and Mies van der Rohe. The group of U of M students extolled the virtues of the province's earliest buildings, like St. Andrew's Anglican Church of 1849 whose "simple plan and form [were] honestly expressed in native limestone." In St. Boniface, the Roman Catholic Cathedral, also of limestone, "was a simple and sane product of its environment."

But according to their ideology things got dicier with the arrival of the Canadian Pacific Railway in the early 1880s. In describing an elaborate Second Empire row housing complex in Winnipeg, the authors noted that it was "an example of a vain attempt to copy the elaborately overdecorated style of architecture." The Legislative Building "was at its best when seen silhouetted against an evening sky, and the applied classic detail cannot be seen. The building then takes on a most impressive monumentality with its large simple mass, horizontal in character, climaxed by the dominating verticality of the tower."

In fact, the whole fifty-year period from 1900 to 1950 was dismissed as an "unusual period," and later labeled the "Grand Detour." The writers observed that designers appeared "to have traveled a circuitous route through phases of imitation, of shallow speculation and experimentation."

Hope, for the group, arrived during the Depression. The students noted that architects had suffered, like many others, the pains of unemployment and therefore were compelled to rethink their work. "Survival lay in creating simple, straightforward, efficient architecture." In discussing the Civic Auditorium of 1932 they observed that "the characteristic features of this style were the plain wall surfaces, large simple masses, large scale and little or no detail." In a telling codex they went on to argue that such a building "was the true expression of a country were the horizon is unbroken and where the distances are so great that small scale and needless detail are incongruous."

For them, the Auditorium marked a return to sanity. And in their appraisal of the building they added another element to their definition of what constitutes a good building: the local. They were rightly proud that the expressive architecture of the modern movement in Canada appeared first in the grain elevator—that is, to a purely Western building. As they noted, "to Le Corbusier and other European critics, the grain elevator (actually, the grain silo) represented the magnificent first fruits of

a new age, making use of the new elements resulting from the engineer's calculations. With their simple, unadorned and functional forms, they became characteristic of a new direction." They asked, hopefully, "Can we expect to find an expression of the prairies, of the dignity and the progressive spirit of its people, through the use of local building materials? Materials such as tyndall stone, most handsome when used in the broad wall surfaces."

In scores of buildings that followed during the late 1950s and throughout the 1960s, the authors of Red River Skyline would have been proud of their colleagues' accomplishments. And none of these was more important than Winnipeg's Civic Centre, a powerful and important symbol of modern architecture at the very heart of the city.

Discussion began in 1948 concerning the merits of building a new City Hall for Winnipeg. It was not until the late 1950s, however, that a national competition brought the issue closer to reality. Ninety-nine entries were considered (the winner is seen on the opposite page), but the results were declined and it would be another four years before a design was selected, and construction began. The building that rose was designed by Green, Blankstein and Russell (better known now as GBR), and ultimately cost $8.2 million. In their design, the architects created a subtle and sophisticated interpretation of the International style, with a distinctly Prairie flavour. Various functions were separated into distinct buildings, with the council chambers on the left and the administrative offices in the seven-storey block on the right.

OTHER TRIES

*Different schemes for a new city hall in Winnipeg
have been contemplated over the years. Plans were
afoot as early as 1912 to replace the 1886 landmark
with a new building. The project never materialized,
however, as a declining economy shifted political
attention to other issues. Perhaps in an effort to ease
voters' disappointment, Mayor T.R. Deacon observed
that the time had passed for building city halls "with
all those pillars around them."*

*The decision in the late 1950s to build a new
Winnipeg Civic Centre at one point called for a
building, right, that would have been placed on a site
directly north of the Legislative Building. Both the
Premier of the day, Duff Roblin, and Winnipeg's
Mayor, Stephen Juba, opposed this siting, and the new Civic Centre rose on the site of the old city hall. The
Premier likely reacted to what would have been a major distraction from the Legislative Building, and the
Mayor was said to be concerned that moving the centre of civic life would only encourage further
decentralization of the city. Whatever the reasons, we should probably be grateful that the space in front of the
Legislature was allowed to remain a simple expanse of green park.*

STEINBACH CITY HALL

*The same year that saw the City of Winnipeg's Civic Centre opened was the same year that
witnessed the completion of a design for a new Municipal Hall for the Town of Steinbach.
Smaller, naturally, and more modest architecturally, the Steinbach building was no less
important for the community. Where other small town councils were making do with their
old spaces, or moving into locally important historic buildings, a few chose to build new.
As Steinbach Mayor Leonard Barkman observed at the time, "this was a progressive step
for the community." A local architect, Norman Reimer, produced a building that was
both dramatic and dignified. At a cost of $175,000 it was an impressive outlay for the
conservative Mennonite community, which had recently occupied the former post office.
But the most impressive thing might have been how open-minded the community was,
to a new form of architecture, and a new way of expressing civic pride.*

Richardson Building

PORTAGE AND MAIN is one of Canada's best known intersections, and for Winnipeggers the corner is distinguished by the city's first modern skyscraper, the Richardson Building. A product of a wealthy and revered Winnipeg family, the 32-storey tower was for many years a symbol of the new Winnipeg: modern and proud. It's impossible to imagine the corner without it. But for years, this prime piece of real estate was home to the humble Marathon Blue Gas Garage.

For several years in the 1930s and 1940s, Marathon Blue Gas capitalized on this strategic corner, and did a brisk business. It is certainly odd to imagine that such a prime piece of real estate, at such a strategic and famous corner, could be so under-utilized. But of course, the bustle of today's automobiles, office towers and business dress belie the fluid veneer of cityscapes.

Before the turn of the twentieth century, the intersection of Portage and Main was merely one of several important junctions in an area that was defined by grand banks and elegant office buildings. The block that now contains the Richardson Building was a typical element in this urban fabric. The northern corner contained three bank buildings while the southern half was populated with small-scale companies. But all that changed in 1905 when the T. Eaton Company chose to build its gigantic new department store farther west on Portage Avenue, and the corner of Portage and Main was dramatically changed. Almost immediately the "T" formed by the intersection of Main Street and Portage Avenue advanced strategically from the location of the Eaton's enterprise and became prime real estate. Naturally, the buildings that occupied the apex of the Portage and Main property lots gained immense new prominence in the city, as they were visible for blocks down Portage Avenue.

The burgeoning grain-trading firm, J.R. Richardson and Company quickly realized the potential in the site. In fact, the Richardsons had proposed to build on the site in the late 1920s, and had called upon Arthur Stoughton to prepare a design for the lot. The stock market crash of 1929, however, dashed their dreams and it would be another 40 years before the family could proceed with its dream.

The booming 1960s offered a new generation of Richardsons the opportunity to fulfill the family ambition. On July 11, 1967, construction on the $15-million building commenced and a little more than two and a half years later, in early November of 1969, a golden bucket was used to hoist the last load of concrete to the top. A formal opening ceremony was held on November 14, 1969, and the J.R. Richardson Building assumed its position as the anchor and beacon at the centre of the city.

During the 1930s and 1940s the Marathon Blue Gas Garage occupied Winnipeg's most prestigious commercial site. The little Tudor Revival station must have been, in its own way, a landmark in the city.

The design that was prepared in the late 1960s by the Winnipeg firm of Smith, Carter, Searle Architects (later known simply as Smith Carter), fit comfortably within the tradition of the International style. The rigorous design tenets of the style can generally be read in the Richardson Building, which is a simple and powerful geometric form, unadorned by applied ornament, with the basic structural system expressed in the slender columns that soar into the sky, and in the repetitious pattern of windows that surround every side. The apparent simplicity of the building aboveground was a structural contrast compared with what went on underground. In a record for the time, 64 mammoth concrete caissons were sunk into the famed Red River gumbo, down to bedrock, to ensure that the building up top would stay put, and straight.

BUILDING FOR JAMES RICHARDSON & SONS LTD.

ANOTHER WAY

In 1929 Arthur Stoughton, Dean of the School of Architecture at the University of Manitoba, was called upon by the Richardsons to draw up a scheme for a major building at Portage and Main. His design was for a 14-storey Art Deco block with a dramatic corner tower whose face would be visible all the way up Portage Avenue. It was this orientation—providing for maximum visibility—that would eventually find expression in the building that finally rose in the 1960s.

DIFFERENT, BUT EQUAL

In building design, you can go up, or you can go across. The Richardsons went tall, with a landmark 32-storey structure that created 219,000 square feet of floor space. Between 1957 and 1959, the Great-West Life Insurance Company put up its new headquarters, across the street from the Legislative Building, and produced a building of, oddly enough, exactly the same size: 219,000 square feet. The low configuration of this building was dependent on a spacious lot size—eight acres— and also on the fact that, being a direct neighbour of the Legislative Building required that it not overshadow that premier symbol of the province. Architects Morani and Morris, from Toronto, produced a design of profound and subtle charms, and one that slowly grows on you. At first glance a simple symmetrical block, the façade was actually composed with two main walls that were on slightly different planes. This misalignment sets up a quiet dissonance, and also creates space on the right-hand side for a low section that reinforces the sense of the building as a set of blocks. At the centre of the composition are a set of stepped blocks, beginning with a low entrance vestibule, then a five-storey stair block and topped with a tall block that actually contains the corporate boardroom. The glazing patterns in the stair block and in the face of the crowning block are excellent examples of the design aesthetic of the period, as espoused by visual artists, especially ones like Piet Mondrian, a Dutch artist whose simple rectilinear designs had been very influential a few decades earlier. The building also exhibits a quiet sophistication in its colours, with the main walls clad in light grey Manitoba limestone contrasted with tangy red granite from Minnesota. The Great-West Life Building is one of the finest buildings constructed in Manitoba in the 1950s.

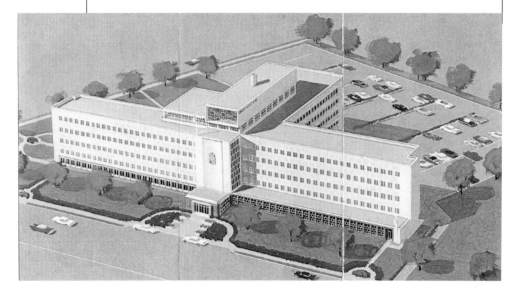

Winnipeg Art Gallery

NOT SINCE THE COMPETITION to design the Legislative Building in 1911 was there such a burst of architectural optimism as greeted the 1969 commission to design Winnipeg's new art gallery. One hundred and nine firms made the short list, and the jurors for the competition considered designs from many heavyweights in the field. However since jurors were never told who the competing architects were, to ensure that they would not select the best known firms or architects (a longstanding and current practice for commissions), the ultimate winner was chosen solely on the merits of the design.

When the formal announcement about the winner was made it must have shocked the architectural elite, jurors, other competitors, the public, and even the winner—Gustavo da Roza, an unheralded young architect teaching at the University of Manitoba. In its comments on da Roza's design, the jury noted that it was "one of the finest, if not the greatest, triangular building designs yet achieved."

Its bold and basic triangularity certainly was to become its claim to fame, but da Roza observed that the choice of form was dictated as well from a practical point of view—in the design process he tried out a variety of more conventional rectilinear schemes to accommodate the program requirement for a footprint of 25,000 square feet, and ultimately found the triangular shape to be the most practical.

In Winnipeg, the result was viewed by some critics as a modern fortress, imposing and cold. But for admirers the Winnipeg Art Gallery (commonly called the WAG) was viewed as sleek, powerful and graceful. This was especially true when the Gallery was contrasted with its most impressive neighbour, the stately Legislative Building, Manitoba's grandest architectural achievement, for which the nearby gallery was a perfect complement and a welcome foil. But the WAG also found itself in the company of a collection of historic buildings that rival the city's Exchange District, with its cluster of historical warehouses and banks. Arrayed in the WAG neighbourhood are such important landmarks as the Law Courts, the Manitoba Archives, the Hudson's Bay Company Store and the Great-West Life Company Building.

The perspective drawing from Gustavo da Roza's winning entry package shows the Winnipeg Art Gallery in all its sharp, crisp angularity. The building is often described as a ship, a great grey hull knifing northward through the flat, golden prairie. While that image has its appeal, it is perhaps too literal, and too limiting. Designed at a time when abstraction in art was in full swing, it is more profitable to consider the sheets of light grey walls in the light of concerns for pattern and form, and the feelings these apparently simple qualities can evoke. And da Roza was meticulous in the actual composition of each facet of the two main walls. After spending some time in the limestone quarries at Garson, he specified a less wasteful cutting procedure to ensure the extraction of the stones he wanted.

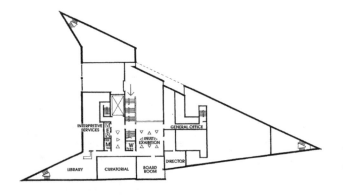

The apparently simple triangular shape of the Winnipeg Art Gallery disguises the skillfully compounded floor plan—in this case the mezzanine gallery spaces on the second level—where the shape turns out to be more jagged and features a variety of wall planes. In fact, the walls of the Gallery are also slightly tilted so as to create different colour tones on the exterior surfaces at various times of the day.

Cultural institutions have increasingly become powerful symbols of a community's maturity, innovation, optimism and of course of their sophistication. Winnipeg has become known across Canada as a proud supporter of the arts and various other cultural activities, and the construction of major buildings to house these functions has produced several landmark buildings in the city. The three featured here sum up important trends in design theory over the course of the past 30 years, as Winnipeg architects sought to express their own sophistication.

MANITOBA CENTENNIAL CONCERT HALL

A consortium of three major Winnipeg architectural firms—Smith, Carter with Moody, Moore and GBR—undertook the design of the city's first major cultural facility of the post-World War II era. Completed in 1967, the Manitoba Centennial Concert Hall was part of a radical urban renewal scheme that saw the elimination of several blocks on either side of Main Street and the construction of various major civic and cultural institutions. The Concert Hall took pride of place, across the street from the new Winnipeg Civic Centre. In this aerial rendering the architects' vision was clearly expressed, with the building's quiet drama and power created through basic shapes, simple colour contrasts, and at the front through the creation of a central wall of windows and hoods whose novel design created a shimmering dance between light and shadow in the lobby area.

MANITOBA THEATRE CENTRE

Just three years after the Centennial Concert Hall was finished, work commenced down the street on a new theatre centre. The designers of the building—Number Ten Architectural Group, A.H. Waisman, Architect and M. Kirby Designer—used a very different architectural vocabulary for their commission. In a style that came to be called Brutalism, the architects created a building that celebrated the elemental qualities inherent especially in exposed concrete, large window openings and, inside, in exposed mechanical systems.

ROYAL CANADIAN MINT

It's not a cultural building, although it could be mistaken for one, set as it is like a jewel in a swath of soft grass. In fact it's the Royal Canadian Mint, opened in 1975 and since that day one of the city's modern landmarks. When it opened the Mint was commissioned to produce coins for Brazil, Israel, Indonesia, Iran and Thailand, as well as its most common denomination, the Canadian penny. In fact, at that time penny production accounted for nearly 60% of the coinage produced. It is perhaps for that reason that Manitoba architect Etienne Gaboury selected a coppery hue for the glass that defined the building's distinct crystalline shape.

Wolfrom Engineering Building

IT IS A BIT OF A CLICHÉ that engineers and architects have a testy relationship with each other, one group of professionals being told that they can't do that (the engineer speaking to the architect), the other group that they shouldn't do that (the architect lecturing the engineer). However, the collaboration between Daniel Wolfrom, a structural engineer, and architect David Penner, in the design of Wolfrom's 1996 office building, proves how meaningless this cliché can be.

In nearly every way this building is a treatise on the subject of civil engineering—that is, how to make buildings and other structures stand up, as efficiently and elegantly as possible. This dialogue is first accomplished by the placement of forms and features in the Wolfrom building. Walls that we think should be nice and straight, actually slope dramatically, even dangerously. Roofs, which are supposed to slope, in this context seem to hang precariously. A large white cube appears to be suspended in mid-air, and is, like other surfaces, raked at odd angles. The cube's street-facing window mirrors the dynamic tension throughout the whole building, being top heavy in its outline. While it's more than a little discomforting in its logic, it is thrilling to look at.

Inside, large support columns are also skewed from plumb, suggesting that the floors above could slump at any minute. Indeed, almost every form and detail makes you aware of the structural dynamism of the building. At the same time it is so obviously stable that the design goes well beyond just sleight of hand to make you experience these opposing feelings.

As one final touch, Penner designed a little suspension bridge just outside the front doors. Like any good suspension bridge this one jiggles with every step, and at the end of the bridge a column forces you to twist your body to get into the building. It's one more device to reinforce the notion that the building is not just a powerful visual commentary about engineering and architecture, but a physical one as well.

In a meeting of the minds, architect David Penner and his client, engineer Daniel Wolfrom, found common ground not only in the design of Wolfrom's office building, but also in the approach to the actual building materials. For both men, the prospect of recycling materials had a deep appeal. As a structural engineer, and with ready access to left-over building materials, Wolfrom found the prospect of re-using perfectly good materials irresistible—and cost-effective of course. For Penner the appeal of recycling was grounded in his approach to the practice of architecture—that while responsive to new ideas and new forms, architects should also celebrate old materials that still have plenty of life left in them. Thus a cursory examination of the building reveals, among a whole host of examples, columns that are actually sewer pipe recycled from other sites, as well as roof joists and maple flooring that were salvaged from buildings that were being renovated.

ALLOWAY RECEPTION CENTRE, FORT WHYTE CENTRE

Architects Dean Syverson and Tom Monteyne also looked to the dramatic potential inherent in the display of physical forces in the design of their addition to the Fort Whyte Centre, south of Winnipeg. Here, we see a visually thrilling jumble of zigzagging, sloped walls, jagged roof planes, and deep beams that jut randomly and ominously above it all. The architects have said that the building is meant to tell the story of tectonic activity at the site, with its dynamic soil

pressures heaving up a structure that is barely held together. That story is evident in the adroit disposition of elements and details. But there is another story here, or at least, an homage. The inordinately long stone wall that defines the north face of the complex, a sophisticated bit of design and engineering, recalls the dry-laid stone walls that delineate property lines and raised floor beds in many a suburban yard. And while the stones look simply placed, anyone who has spent a few weekends creating their own masterpiece will immediately appreciate the immense skill and care with which the masons undertook their task.

Red River College: Princess Street Campus

FOR ALMOST 20 YEARS a set of historically important Victorian commercial buildings on Princess Avenue in Winnipeg sat abandoned, and decaying, home to pigeons and rats. These buildings, the last remnants of a once-vibrant commercial area around Winnipeg's old city hall, had been identified by the City as worthy of preservation. And while the City ensured through the years that the buildings did not actually fall down, it appeared only a matter of time before lack of interest and neglect would render them irredeemable.

Hope for the buildings came from the 1997 designation of the area in which they stand—the Exchange District—as a National Historic Site. That federal distinction created a heritage-friendly climate that promised the buildings a potential new lease on life. But it did not provide for any practical resolutions for how that new life would unfold. That kind of resolution came from Red River College, which identified the site as a perfect downtown place to create a satellite home for several of its most cutting-edge programs—Media and Information Technology.

But there was one problem. The College actually needed a different facility than was offered by the existing heritage buildings, which were simply too small and awkward to accommodate the complex needs of the faculty's program, and the estimated 2,000 students and 200 staff it would house. After a good deal of debate it was decided to preserve the five façades, along with some special interior finishes, but to remove the crumbling and unstable sections behind. In their place would rise a new building.

And not just any run-of-the-mill building. While meeting the College's needs, it also had to conform with the heritage character of the Exchange District, and thus to a nineteenth century warehouse aesthetic. The solution prepared by architects Corbett Cibinel was for a building that recalled the form of such structures, but with a whole new material – rather than monolithic brick walls, a more modern and appropriate skin of glass.

It is this kind of project—where a new building responds to an older one with respect, but not deference—that may become more common in the future. Having lost so many fine historic buildings in the 1960s and 1970s in Winnipeg and other major Canadian centres, projects like Red River College Campus, slated for completion late in 2003, show that it is possible to create a viable and usable harmony between old and new.

THE BOOM THAT DIDN'T CRASH

The dainty Victorian façades on the south side of the complex were already a little tipsy when construction on the new Red River Campus began. When they were built, in the early 1880s, Winnipeg's real estate market was being wildly driven by speculation over the new pan-Canada railway, the CPR. Not surprisingly, buildings in Winnipeg were being slapped up willy-nilly to accommodate rapid growth, and several of the Princess Street buildings were so poorly constructed it is a marvel that they lasted at all. In the determination to preserve them, it was necessary to brace the delicate facades with great steel buttresses that improbably held the long wall plane up for several months as work proceeded underneath and behind them.

The Red River College Princess Street Campus, and its architects, Corbett Cibinel, have been recognized with a bevy of awards. Most prominent was its selection as one of the three representatives for Canada in the Green Building Challenge held in Oslo, Norway in 2002. That ongoing annual competition seeks to promote in the building industry ways to measure and evaluate a building's energy and environmental performance. The goal is to ensure that more buildings contribute to global sustainability by conserving natural resources and minimizing energy use. More and more architects in Manitoba are heeding this clarion call. For their entry, Corbett Cibinel identified a welter of "green" aspects of the Red River College project, the primary one being the preservation of the historic facades, but also including highly technical approaches to the whole design. From the recycling of building materials, to solutions for dealing with greenhouse gases and limiting emissions of ozone-deleting substances, the architects kept their eyes at all times on opportunities to make the complex one of the cleanest, most environmentally friendly buildings in the world.

APPENDIX

Researching Your Own Home

TRACING A BUILDING'S HISTORY, and telling its stories, can be a quest that is both satisfying and fascinating. The search for facts and stories, however, is often a daunting undertaking. Many beginner researchers simply don't know where to look for information about a building's past. Or else they get started, but are discouraged when historical information seems difficult to access or find.

This section is a brief overview that will help point beginners in the right directions in seeking answers about a building's history. It should help you avoid the time, energy and expense of looking for the wrong information in the wrong places. The more pleasant the experience is, the more likely it is to be successful. Beginners may find that what begins as a modest quest—looking for a construction date, the name of an original owner—may also serve as a launching pad or as inspiration to go on to research broader historical issues.

Getting There

STARTING OUT

There are as many reasons to research a building as there are buildings. To abate curiosity, to help ensure proper renovations, to help understand the past and to learn about the people who once lived, worked or worshipped in a building, are just some of the typical reasons to contemplate a journey into research, and into the past. Still, each and every building has its own unique story to tell, and studying its particular history helps us understand its situation today.

Simply researching a building lends itself to an appreciation of just how much work went into constructing a building and, at the same time, can extend to answer questions about a particular area or an era. While the end result of finding answers to questions may be satisfying, the process can be as well. And as you look for information in archives, libraries and museums, you may find beauty in the peace of those places.

BEGIN WITH WORDS

A good place to start researching is at the local library. By perusing books, newspapers, and magazines about a certain time and place, you will be able to frame the types of questions you will need to ask in your research. In addition, you will broaden your knowledge of a particular time and place in general, which will help you contextualize and understand the information you gather.

Depending on the scope of your project, you may wish to read basic architectural books to help you identify certain architectural styles, trends and terminology. Books, newspapers and periodicals on local architecture, history, culture and events can illustrate the types of questions that other researchers have asked when approaching their subject. As you discover what others have asked, write down your own questions.

PLOT AND PLAN

While the idea of planning seems obvious, many researchers often start out without a clear plan, wasting both time and money. You will need to determine ahead of time the specific records that you need to search, and locate where they are stored. A good idea is to always phone ahead and talk to research staff about the kind of work you are undertaking and what kind of information you are trying to track down. Relying on the help of professionals can also help you gauge whether or not your approach is correct, and if enough existing materials exists to make your research project worthwhile.

While most archivists or record searchers are helpful, they will appreciate it if you know what you are looking for. Also, you can expect most archivists to point you in the right direction, but don't expect them to do basic searching for you.

Prior to heading out, enquire about hours of operation, as many archives and government offices feature limited hours of operation. You may also want to ask if you can receive photocopies of certain records or photographs, as some institutions do not allow the photocopying of archival data.

If what you are studying is part of a larger project, it is worthwhile to contact government agencies or local historical associations to discuss your plans. Record the names of those people you contact, just in case you need to refer to them later.

Scope and size of project will vary according to both personal need for information and inspiration. If you are undertaking research because you want to place a new addition on your house, the size and scope of your project could be more condensed than if you lived in a historical mansion and wanted to restore it to its former glory. In some cases, the boundaries of investigation will be obvious right from the start. Conversely, if you are interested in researching a building because you have heard it is haunted, your research project can be a small or large scale as your time, energy and personal commitment warrants.

THE DETECTIVE WORK

In most cases you are trying to gather the raw materials required to piece together a larger picture of the past. Gather all of the pictures and plans that you can, and wherever you go make sure you take along a notebook to record your findings. Copy information just as you find it.

All documents and images will require some level of interpretation. Understanding their specific function will help you interpret the values and purpose that their creators had in mind, and much consideration should be given to particular bias. With newspaper articles, for example, it is often worthwhile to know as much about the journalist and publisher as it is the topic you are researching. Invariably the individual perception of the author or creator can be sensed and measured. Be sensitive as well to the historical times in which the documents or images were made, and try to evaluate the times when assessing the work.

Accuracy must also be considered. Hand drawn maps, measurements, grammar and spelling of names could bear inaccuracies. By scrutinizing the information carefully, considering when it was prepared, and under what circumstances, may help you assess the accuracy of the work.

If you find the historical work of researching a building fascinating, your scope may creep well beyond your original intent. You may begin by looking into what a building's original purpose was and then find that you are equally interested in the inhabitants of the building. What did they do? Where did they work? What was their financial status? What was the surrounding land used for? You may find that you enjoy research for its own sake and continue to extend it into exploring local history or tracing your ancestry.

PAINTING A BIGGER PICTURE

Researching buildings can help you reconstruct the community and culture of a certain time, and also understand the people and personalities that inhabited them. Don't be surprised if your work takes you far beyond the building. For example, your research may be enhanced if you understand significant events. These can involve anything from the Great Depression to World War II to the advent of the automobile and the development of suburbs. Add to this the knowledge of home life, construction standards, occupations, trade and industry, local laws, the role of the church in a community, leisure activities of the day, and lifestyles of the rich and poor. By significantly broadening the scope of your research you will garner greater insights into the history of buildings.

If your research takes you beyond your original scope, you can turn to many of the same resource sources identified in this book to bolster your general understanding.

PRESERVING THE EVIDENCE

After you have completed your research you will probably want to review the materials, place them in context and compile what you have discovered in some form of central product or directory. Your original goals and perhaps even your ambitions will define how far you want to go with your materials.

If you have undertaken a significant research project for a major historical building or buildings, you may wish to compile your information in manuscript format and seek publication through a professional book publisher. If your research was intended for personal use only, you may want to simply record your notes and paste photocopies in an album, or you may want to forward it to a local archive. Regardless, however, of how you intend to use your research, here are some fundamentals that you will want to ensure are implemented:

- Record the source of all information and the date you found the information.

- Record the information both on paper and electronically if you have access to a computer. In paper or electronic format ensure that you have duplicates and ask a friend or family member to store a copy of the original. Place your originals in a safety deposit, or fireproof box. Images should be duplicated and also stored, as should originals.

- Notes should be duplicated exactly as they were originally written. Do not "ad lib," abbreviate or omit anything.

- Transcribe your notes shortly after you record them. The longer you delay the procedure the more chance you will misinterpret your notes.

- Keep all records and information in a single binder prior to compilation and regularly make copies of everything you are storing.

- If you are acquiring numerous records, use a card filing system or separators to help you sort your work.

- When interviewing, produce clear, comprehensive notes, or ask if you can tape record the interviewee.

- If other published research exists, which you wish to incorporate into your own written documents, be sure to credit the original source.

- If you are submitting your work for publication it is wise to ask about contracts and copyright issues. Also, consider your audience when transcribing and writing your work.

- Don't be brief. The more detail and information you provide the better.

- Write clearly, use correct grammar and check spelling.

- Ensure your work is objective and reflects as little bias as possible.

Recovering the Evidence

THE BUILDING

The best place to begin researching a building is with the building itself. The building materials, construction techniques, style (see "Styles of Architecture in Manitoba," following), room disposition, etc., are all interesting avenues for investigation, and for discovering key pieces of information. Of course it is also possible that the building also holds other kinds of information—old newspapers, documents, letters—that can be used for answering certain questions.

ORAL EVIDENCE AND INTERVIEWING SUGGESTIONS

Learning more about buildings from the memories of those who can provide them can be one of the most rewarding forms of research. Talking to the right people can prove invaluable. In the case of houses, this can be as easy as locating people who knew former residents or who have lived in the area for a long time. They can often provide clues that will augment further investigation such as significant names, dates, alterations and renovation information. In addition, they can provide hard-to-come-by eye witness evidence. While casual conversation can often be the source of informal research, if you are looking for more substantive information it is best to be prepared. Make sure you prepare a list of questions in advanced and compare the answers to other information that you have garnered. A good resource on how to conduct interviews exist at the Manitoba Museum of Man and Nature and is titled, *Oral History, Basic Techniques.*

Written Evidence and Where to Find It

DIRECTORIES

Directories are basically lists of street addresses and the names of occupants. The best known directory in Manitoba is the Henderson Directory, usually housed in public libraries. In Winnipeg, the Centennial Library has a collection of Henderson Directories dating back to the 1880s. Henderson's, as they are more commonly known, can provide information about a person's occupation and, when reviewed in sequence can also suggest approximate building construction dates. A challenge with many directories is that the information can be inaccurate or incomplete. They also tend to be published a year later than the information was gathered, so they can be out date. Also, watch for street name changes. Other directories also exist and many are published through trade associations. If a commercial building was associated with a particular trade, you may find some details about it in dated trade association listings.

NEWSPAPERS

Old newspapers offer a rich journey into the past. While they occasionally will include information about particular buildings, especially important local construction projects, they are perhaps more useful for creating a context for your research. Information about local events and personalities will allow you to place your building against a real and vibrant backdrop. It is important to remember that newspapers were once highly partisan enterprises, politically, and that certain papers will not include information about political opponents. The Legislative Library of Manitoba maintains a large collection of newspapers on microfilm.

LAND TITLES DOCUMENTS

If Henderson's directories (above) are not available for your community, or if the information in them is not deemed accurate enough, it is possible to search land titles to get a list of property owners. It is important to realize that no land titles documents actually identify buildings, and thus will not provide construction dates. Moreover, land title searches can be expensive, depending on the number of titles recovered.

BUILDING PERMITS

In the early 20th century, Winnipeg and other urban centres began to require builders to submit information on their proposed project. These building permits ensured that new buildings attained an acceptable level of safety. Permits are invaluable records that can contain information on materials, costs, designers and builders. While certain jurisdictions will have endeavoured to maintain these records, don't be surprised or disappointed if you cannot trace down the particular permit you need.

ANNUAL REPORTS, BULLETINS AND PERIODICALS

Usually associated with large corporations and governments, these materials often provide detailed information about the building projects undertaken by those entities. The best place to start looking is at the organization's head office or its public relations office. Many government annual reports are preserved at the Legislative Library of Manitoba.

Pictorial Evidence and Where to Find It

Photographs, illustrations and technical drawings contain potentially useful information. But they can be a disappointing route for many researchers; most buildings were not the subject for any of these media. Those lucky enough to discover old images, however, will find them endlessly interesting, and useful in building research.

PHOTOGRAPHS

Historic, or archival, photographs are a vital record of a building's original state. Photographs of public and private business buildings are usually easier to locate than those of houses. While pictures of the outside of buildings abound in public collections, interior shots are harder to find. The Provincial Archives of Manitoba and the Western Canadian Pictorial Index have impressive collections of historic photographs.

Winnipeg's Richardson Building

PICTURES AND ILLUSTRATIONS

Artistic renditions of buildings and landscapes are uncommon, but exceptions can be found and can provide helpful clues in determining landscape changes and renovations. Paintings, drawings and lithographic prints may prove helpful, especially for researching periods when cameras were not widely used. In all cases, renditions are interpretative and generally express the aesthetic vision of the artist. It is important to scrutinize them carefully as they contain embellishments or deletions based on personal taste.

TECHNICAL DRAWINGS

Technical drawings are more likely to be found for large-scale projects, where professional architects and draftsmen were employed to address the complexities of construction through series of clear, technical drawings. Prior to attempting to track down technical drawings, first assess whether or not there was an architect associated with the building's design. For large projects, many drawings were rendered, including cross-sections, floor plans, elevations, and a welter of detail drawings. A blueprint is the process used to creating technical drawings, and not a specific category of technical drawing.

Maps and Plans and Where to Find Them

PARISH PLANS

Named for the boundaries of Roman Catholic and Anglican parishes, these plans depict thin, long strips of land, commonly referred to as river lots. The lots stretched backward from waterways such as the Red and Assiniboine, as most landowners required access to two vital resources that rivers provided: water and transportation. The City of Winnipeg was surveyed into river lots. Available at the Provincial Archives of Manitoba, parish plans will provide an excellent overview of the lot you may be researching, although the location of buildings was not always marked. Correlating the river lot number in a particular parish with various written parish records will reveal the name of the original owner of the lot.

TOWNSHIP PLANS

In 1870 the Federal Government commenced its survey of most of Manitoba into huge square townships. The plans that were produced in this impressive undertaking are available at the Provincial Archives of Manitoba. Township plans will provide a researcher with a good sense of historical landscape, where some pioneer buildings were placed, topography, homesteaders' names, waterways, vegetation, farming activities and land quality. If you know the section, township and range numbers (the co-ordinates), you can correlate the township plan to a township file, and ascertain the original owners of the land.

CIVIC PLANS

Civic plans outline legal property divisions in communities. Plans of cities and large scale town plans can be a useful adjunct to other maps and guides. Generally compiled by city planners and professional map-makers, they are often the most formal record of development patterns, and list lots, blocks and the names of streets. Early civic plans can be compared to recent ones, which will indicate if changes have occurred over time.

FIRE INSURANCE PLANS

An impressive collection of fire insurance plans from 1917 has been collected and is maintained at the Provincial Archives of Manitoba. These highly detailed renderings, featuring building sizes and locations, building materials, wall heights, room functions, furnace types and heating systems, were used to assess fire risks. The plans are fascinating, and reliable, renderings of communities.

Styles of Architecture in Manitoba

Certain of the buildings featured in this book are virtual textbook examples of the most popular styles of architecture employed in Manitoba between 1870 and 1940. The following list identifies those styles, describes some of the key characteristics, and notes the examples contained on previous pages. Please note that many buildings were built without reference to any style, or with only a modest application of certain features or details of a style. Thus don't be surprised or disappointed if you can't fit your building into any of these categories.

GEORGIAN (1820-1970)

The Georgian was most popular in Great Britain during the reign of the first three King Georges (1714 to 1820) from which it derives its name. A vernacular interpretation of the style, in which detail was minimized, became a very popular architectural expression throughout Great Britain. In Manitoba, where the vernacular tradition was used, it was closely associated with the buildings of the Hudson's Bay Company and those built by Company employees who retired to the Red River Settlement.

Examples: Twin Oaks (page 12), Grey Nuns' Convent (page 11)

GOTHIC REVIVAL (1850-1900)

The Gothic Revival was one of the most enduring and influential architectural movements of the 19th century. Based on a revival of medieval architecture, especially that of England and France, it passed through successive phases and influenced most building types. However, in Manitoba the style is mainly identified with church architecture and is often defined by the pointed arch. Many Gothic Revival buildings have steep gable roofs highlighted with intricate details.

Examples: St. Andrew's and St. Peter's Anglican churches (pages 54 and 55), Holy Trinity Anglican Church (page 56), Grund Lutheran Church (page 59), Kennedy House (page 13)

SECOND EMPIRE (1880-1890)

Introduced to Canada and the United States from France via England, this style takes its name from the French Second Empire, the reign of Napoleon III (1852-1870). It was commonly used for public buildings, but also for houses and educational institutions. The Roman Catholic church adopted this style for its convents and schools.

Examples: Government House (page 16), Old Legislative Building (page 50), Old Court House (page 51), Bohémier House (page 30)

ITALIANATE (1880-1900)

This style was loosely based on the Renaissance villas of Italy, which were characterized by a low pedimented roof and classical detail application.

Examples: Birks Building (page 85), Brandon Fire Station (page 47)

ROMANESQUE REVIVAL (1885-1905)

Originally little more than an offshoot of the Gothic Revival, it was distinguished by the use of typically Romanesque motifs, including the round arch and decorative patterns. In its later phase, American architect H.H. Richardson (1828-1886) created his own unique interpretation which became the model for a North American Romanesque-based style.

Examples: Dominion Post Office (page 49), Dalnavert (page 18), St. Boniface Cathedral (page 66), St. Mary's Roman Catholic Cathedral (page 57)

QUEEN ANNE REVIVAL (1890-1910)

In North America this definition, originally based on buildings from the reign in England of Queen Anne (1702-1714), was loosely applied to describe an eclectic style which incorporated architectural elements borrowed from a variety of historical periods. In Manitoba, the style had its greatest effect on residential design.

Examples: Pile of Bones Villa, Ross House, Sutherland House, McFadden House (pages 24 and 25)

CLASSICAL REVIVAL (1900-1930)

This revival was based on the classical forms of ancient Greece and Rome. In its simplest form it was referred to as Neo-Classical and usually followed simple Greek architecture. Beaux-Arts Classicism was named after the Parisian architecture school *Ecole des beaux-arts* and was very popular in the United States. The *Ecole* encouraged designs of a grand nature with a formal and clearly structured arrangement of parts.

Examples: Legislative Building (page 44), Winnipeg CPR Station (page 82), Bank of Montreal (page 86), Hudson's Bay Company Building (page 80)

LATE GOTHIC REVIVAL (1900-1940)

The flamboyant Victorian Gothic architecture of the late 19th century gave way in the early 1900s to a smoother and more subdued style referred to as the Late Gothic Revival. The style was most popularly used for churches, schools and universities. In this context it is often referred to as Collegiate Gothic.

Examples: Minto Armoury (page 48), Tache Hall (page 75)

CHICAGO STYLE (1905-1920)

The Chicago School, or Style, takes its name from the Chicago architects of the 1880s and 90s who took the heavy Romanesque-style warehouse and developed from it the beginnings of the modern skyscraper. Height being an ingredient of the style, it is often called the Commercial style because of its use for office towers.

Examples: Electric Railway Chambers Building (page 89)

ART DECO AND ART MODERNE (1930-1950)

Both Art Deco and Art Moderne buildings were part of the jazz-age, and the Modern movement, which rejected historical eclecticism. Art Deco was most popular in the 1920s and 30s and was distinguished by an emphasis on the smooth cube with hard-edged, low-relief ornament. Art Moderne was popularized during the Great Depression of the 1930s, and was meant to represent the dynamic progress of the 20th century. Its inspiration came from the machine aesthetic of the period's industrial design, especially that of the railway car, motorcar and steamship. Hence it is a very streamlined style, giving through its rounded corners a sense of speed and motion.

Royal Canadian Mint, designed by Etienne Gaboury

Additional Sources of Evidence

Useful Addresses

Winnipeg Centennial Library
251 Donald Street, Winnipeg

Provincial Archives of Manitoba
200 Vaughan Street, Winnipeg

Manitoba Legislative Library
200 Vaughan Street, Winnipeg

Manitoba Historical Society
470-167 Lombard Avenue, Winnipeg

Western Canada Pictorial Index
404-63 Albert Street, Winnipeg

Manitoba Museum of Man and Nature
190 Rupert Avenue, Winnipeg

The World Wide Web

HISTORY SITES

Provincial Archives of Manitoba: http://www.gov.mb.ca/chc/archives/index.html
Manitoba Legislative Library: http://www.gov.mb.ca/chc/leglib_index.html
Manitoba Culture, Heritage and Tourism: http://gov.mb.ca/chc/
The Canadian Association of Professional Heritage Consultants: http://www.caphc.ca/

ARCHITECTURE SITES

World of Old Houses: http://www.oldhoueses.com.au/
Association for Preservation Technology International: http://apti.org/
Old House Journal: http://www.oldhousejournal.com/default.asp
This Old House: http://www.phs.org/wgbh/thisoldhouse.home.html
National Building Museum (United States): http://www.nbm.org/

GENEALOGY SITES

Family Search Internet Genealogy Service: http://www.familysearch.org/
Canadian Genealogy & History: http://www.islandnet.com/~jveinot/cghl/
Genealogical Resources on the Internet (Canada): http://www.personal.umcih.edu/~cgaunt/canada.html
Sources for Genealogical Research in Canada: http://www.igs.net/~bdmlhm/cangenealogy
Association for Gravestone Studies: http://www.gravestonestudies.org/

Case Study

We live in a small house on the banks of the Assiniboine River. Our home features a steep gabled roof and presents more as a country cottage than an inner city house. It's small, unassuming, and not very old. At first glance it is an unlikely repository for any stories worth telling, but still, some have been found.

Upon entry, the foyer walls meet in a beautiful curve, a modest example of Art Moderne styling. This immediately suggests the building's construction date: the 1930s or 40s. Looking at it from the street, it appears simple, but this belies its true façade – that which faces the river, where a high dormered window dominates. Entering the house on the street side foyer allows guests a view of the familiarities of inner city urban life – cars, passersby, overhead wires, back lanes. But if our guests turn their heads ever so slightly, in the opposite direction, they see lush urban nature. Tall white pines, tall-grass prairie and a half acre of ancient riverbed, cut short when it rolls into the Assiniboine.

THE HOUSE

We moved in four years ago and undertook to change the look and feel of our new home. We began by removing a load-bearing wall in our bedroom to make way for a single large room. Our intent was to replace the wall, which separated two bedrooms. This wall would be replaced by a large beam which would be inserted into the ceiling and which would be necessary to support the second floor. Surprisingly, once we removed the wall we found a beam was already in place, along with a false ceiling, and old wires that lead nowhere.

We then began to examine the hardwood floor. It revealed that alterations were made to the floor plan. The ghostly outlines of old walls, still visible on the floor despite a recent refinishing, showed that a wall had once separated living and dining room, and that the main bedroom had originally been two rooms. Looking more closely at stairs leading to the second floor also suggested an early modification; the placement of the bottom stair and ever-so-slightly mismatched baseboards told us that the stairs had been added later.

Why, we wondered, was the beam added? Where did the wires lead? Why was there a false ceiling?

THE YARD

Around the same time, we began gardening in the backyard. While casually digging on the riverbank one afternoon, our shovels kept hitting a hard layer which made digging impossible. We found a pole and spiked it into the area around us to see if we could measure the breadth and depth of the hard layer our shovels kept hitting. After a few spikes it was clear we were not hitting a solitary large rock. We were intrigued. After several hours of moving dirt we unmasked an old terrace made of patterned terra cotta and concrete bricks. At this point we became intrigued by the thought of who might have lived in our house, on this land, before us. Here is what our case study uncovered about our house and one family who lived there before us.

The Investigation

PARISH PLANS

Consulting old parish plans and related documents, we found that the river lot on which our house was located, Number 57 in the Parish of St. James, was originally owned by Henry John Arkland. It was impossible to determine where the Arkland House had been located. Still, it was interesting to contemplate the likelihood of Henry John Arkland standing at the river's edge of our land. An archivist at the Provincial Archives observed that for about a decade between 1875 and 1885, steam boats plied the Assiniboine between Winnipeg and Fort Qu'Appelle in Saskatchewan, and would have passed by this spot regularly. It also occurred to us that it was possible that Native people, perhaps a group of Assiniboine, for whom our river was named, might have camped on what is now our back yard.

CATALOGUES

We were unable to find any original plans or even an old catalogue that featured a similar-looking house. Since the house does not look like any others on the street we speculated that it was a custom job, and we were right. Through a series of interviews and research, we discovered that a neighbour had built the house in 1942 for his daughter who chose not to live here.

DIRECTORIES

To establish who had lived in the house, we looked through Henderson's Directories and discovered that the same couple had lived in the house for almost 50 years. The woman was an artist, her husband a dentist (and we will refer to them as the Held family, not their real name). After the Helds, another family lived in the house briefly, for two years.

PERSONAL INTERVIEWS

A phone call to Mrs. Held, who was now widowed, was revealing and confirmed a great deal about what we had suspected about our house. The Helds had indeed removed walls; the one in the bedroom to create a set of large closets and a vanity. They had added a staircase to the second floor loft, and installed a massive window exposing the loft to fabulous westerly light. The window gave Mrs. Held the light she required for her artwork.

They also loved to entertain in their back yard river lot. Particularly on their terraces. The terrace we uncovered was previously home to the Held's fully-heated, electrically-lit, Japanese pagoda. The Helds were not Japanese but were Jewish, a fact confirmed in conversation with Mrs. Held, and hinted at by the outlines of the *mezuzahs* we found at each door frame. Still, Mrs. Held explained that they loved Japanese design.

The Held yard was apparently gorgeously landscaped in Japanese style, with cedars and yes, those previously mentioned white pines. Many an evening garden party took place on their lavish terrace, before, that is, it was completely obliterated by great flood of 1950. It remained covered in riverbed silt until we began digging and finally, uncovered it, almost 50 years later.

Their love of Japanese design was continued within the home. There, a crew of Japanese carpenters (likely displaced from British Columbia during World War II, given the 1942 construction date) designed and installed veneered, Japanese-inspired cupboards in the small European kitchen. We assume the Helds sought security for certain items, because within the kitchen, we continue to find secret drawers.

NEXT STEPS

Discovering the history of our own home influenced our decisions. We have decided to preserve the original Held terrace and have surrounded it with a Japanese-inspired garden. Additionally, our front yard incorporates Japanese rock garden motifs and our Japanese-style kitchen cupboards will not be replaced with more modern ones.

Knowledge of pre-existing walls and false ceilings has made our own renovations easier and has also influenced all of our renovations, both in terms of structure and design.

Acknowledgements

WE ARE ESPECIALLY GRATEFUL to our publisher and editor Gregg Shilliday of Great Plains Publications and the marketing team of Charmagne de Veer and Jewls Dengl. We also thank the firm of Taylor George Design for the layout and design of this book.

David thanks his colleagues at the Province of Manitoba's Historic Resources Branch who have afforded him the opportunity to extend the hobby he loves, architectural history, into his career. For that he is greatly indebted to Donna Dul and Neil Einarson. Research papers prepared by Randy Rostecki, Elaine Kisiow, Sheila Grover and Murray Peterson also were invaluable in adding important details to many of the building texts. In addition, as the primary researcher for this book, David would like to thank the staff at the Provincial Archives of Manitoba, Legislative Library and the Winnipeg Centennial Library for assisting him when necessary.

We would also like to thank Jasper Devanik Butterfield, who joined our family mid-way through this book and was a storehouse of patience, wit and good temperament. To our parents, our most loyal fans, we are also grateful.

We also want to offer thanks to everyone who helped with this book whose names are omitted here, either because they modestly insisted on anonymity or because of our oversight.

Photo Credits

All photographs in this book are courtesy of the Provincial Archives of Manitoba, except the following:

HOUSES

Page 12: Twin Oaks (after) courtesy Historic Resources Branch
Page 13: Kennedy House (after) courtesy Historic Resources Branch
Page 17: Arthur Meighen House courtesy David Butterfield
Page 18: Dalnavert interior courtesy Historic Resources Branch
Page 20: Margaret Laurence House and interior courtesy Historic Resources Branch; Margaret Laurence courtesy National Film Board of Canada
Page 23: Eaton House courtesy David Butterfield

FARMS

Page 28: Sandison House courtesy Historic Resources Branch
Page 30: Bohémier House courtesy David Butterfield; Barn courtesy Historic Resources Branch
Page 31: Johnson House courtesy David Butterfield
Page 33: Mennonite Housebarn courtesy David Butterfield; Barn detail courtesy Historic Resources Branch
Page 35: Christina Guild House courtesy Historic Resources Branch
Page 37: Fox Farm Tower courtesy David Butterfield
Page 38: Negrycz Farm views courtesy David Butterfield

OFFICIAL

Page 42: Brandon House courtesy Historic Resources Branch
Page 47: Brandon Fire Station courtesy Historic Resources Branch
Page 49: Dominion Post Office, Portage la Prairie courtesy National Archives of Canada

CHURCHES

Page 55: St. Peter's Dynevor Anglican Church courtesy David Butterfield
Page 58: St. Francois Xavier Roman Catholic Church courtesy David Butterfield
Page 59: Grund Lutheran Church views courtesy Historic Resources Branch
Page 61: Emerson Baptist Church courtesy Robert Hill
Page 63: St. Elie Romanian Orthodox Church interior views courtesy Historic Resources Branch
Pages 64,65: Ukrainian Catholic Church of the Immaculate Conception courtesy Historic Resources Branch
Page 66: St. Boniface Cathedral interior courtesy Arlette Hébert

SCHOOLS

Page 71: Union Point School interior courtesy Historic Resources Branch
Page 72: Isaac Brock School and Wolseley School courtesy Winnipeg School Division No. 1
Page 74: Brandon University construction view courtesy Corbett Cibinel Architects

COMMERCIAL

Page 84: Landry General Store courtesy Historic Resources Branch
Page 87: The Northern Bank and Bison detail courtesy David Butterfield

INDUSTRIAL

Page 96: Inglis Grain Elevators courtesy Historic Resources Branch
Page 102: Gunn's Water Mill courtesy David Butterfield

RECREATIONAL

Page 109: Lillian Gish courtesy David Butterfield
Page 111: Darlingford War Memorial courtesy Historic Resources Branch
Page 112: Virden Opera House courtesy David Butterfield